THE U.S. GOVERNMENT
HOW IT WORKS

THE IMPEACHMENT PROCESS

THE U.S. GOVERNMENT
HOW IT WORKS

★ ★ ★

THE CENTRAL INTELLIGENCE AGENCY
THE DEPARTMENT OF HOMELAND SECURITY
THE FEDERAL BUREAU OF INVESTIGATION
THE HISTORY OF THE DEMOCRATIC PARTY
THE HISTORY OF THE REPUBLICAN PARTY
THE HISTORY OF THE THIRD PARTIES
THE HOUSE OF REPRESENTATIVES
HOW A LAW IS PASSED
HOW THE CONSTITUTION WAS CREATED
HOW THE PRESIDENT IS ELECTED
THE IMPEACHMENT PROCESS
THE PRESIDENCY
THE SENATE
THE SUPREME COURT

THE U.S. GOVERNMENT
HOW IT WORKS

THE IMPEACHMENT PROCESS

JOHN MURPHY

An imprint of Infobase Publishing

The Impeachment Process

Copyright © 2007 by Infobase Publishing

All rights reserved. No part of this book may be reproduced or utilized in any form or by any means, electronic or mechanical, including photocopying, recording, or by any information storage or retrieval systems, without permission in writing from the publisher. For information, contact:

Chelsea House
An imprint of Infobase Publishing
132 West 31st Street
New York NY 10001

Library of Congress Cataloging-in-Publication Data

Murphy, John, 1968–
  The impeachment process / John Murphy.
  p. cm. — (The U.S. government : how it works)
  Includes bibliographical references and index.
  ISBN-13: 978-0-7910-9465-5 (hardcover)
  ISBN-10: 0-7910-9465-0 (hardcover)
  1. Impeachments—United States—Juvenile literature. 2. Presidents—United States—Juvenile literature. 3. Impeachments. 4. United States—Politics and government. I. Title. II. Series.

KF5075.Z9M87 2007
342.73'062—dc22   2006100500

Chelsea House books are available at special discounts when purchased in bulk quantities for businesses, associations, institutions, or sales promotions. Please call our Special Sales Department in New York at (212) 967-8800 or (800) 322-8755.

You can find Chelsea House on the World Wide Web at
http://www.chelseahouse.com

Text design by James Scotto-Lavino
Cover design by Ben Peterson

Printed in the United States of America
Bang NMSG 10 9 8 7 6 5 4 3 2 1

This book is printed on acid-free paper.

All links and Web addresses were checked and verified to be correct at the time of publication. Because of the dynamic nature of the Web, some addresses and links may have changed since publication and may no longer be valid.

CONTENTS

1 Introduction 7
2 The Origins of Impeachment 13
3 The Creation of a Federal Impeachment Process 22
4 Impeachment Proceedings in the House of Representatives 38
5 Impeachment Proceedings in the Senate 45
6 Notable Impeachment Proceedings in U.S. History 54
7 The Future of the Impeachment Process 77

Glossary 90
Bibliography 93
Further Reading 95
Picture Credits 97
Index 98

1

Introduction

The impeachment process is one of the most serious and solemn of government proceedings. It can result in the trial and conviction of a president of the United States and immediate removal from office. Despite all the drama, intrigue, and gravity that surround this remarkable judicial process, however, impeachment is poorly understood by most Americans.

Many people believe that the term *impeached* implies that an official has been convicted of the charges brought against him or her. Others believe that a leader who has been impeached has been kicked out of office after having been found guilty. Still others assume that only a president can be impeached. Many Americans are convinced that President Richard Nixon was impeached but that President Bill Clinton was not. None of these beliefs is accurate. Clearly, there is great confusion about just what impeachment is and what "being impeached" means.

Part of the reason that there is so much confusion over the impeachment process is that it has rarely been used in the United States. Americans are unfamiliar with the process's complex legal terms and procedures simply because it has been set into motion very infrequently, especially at the presidential level. This is a testament to the seriousness and responsibility with which impeachment is approached by those who have the power to wield it. It is not a process to enter into lightly, as its consequences for the nation can be dire and destabilizing.

What exactly is impeachment, and what does it mean for an official to be impeached? The best way to understand the impeachment process is to think of it as a trial. Just as in a criminal or civil trial, accusations are made, investigations into wrongdoing are performed, charges are brought, and the "suspect" is tried before a judge and jury. In this case, however, the judge is the chief justice of the United States, the jury members are senators, and the prosecuting attorneys are members of the House of Representatives.

THE BASIC PROCESS

As outlined in the Constitution, the federal impeachment process is startlingly simple and straightforward considering the political turmoil and national chaos that its outcome can produce. Federal officeholders who can be impeached include not only the president but also the vice president and "all civil officers of the United States." Over time, this group has been understood to include federal judges and cabinet members (such as the secretary of

Members of the U.S. House of Representatives Judiciary Committee, investigating grounds for impeachment of President Richard Nixon, start a session on Capitol Hill. Nixon resigned before he could be officially impeached.

defense or the secretary of education), but not senators or House representatives.

The House's Role

The process begins when a member of the House of Representatives, under oath, brings a charge or list of charges against one of these officials. The charges are then referred to the House Judiciary Committee.

The Judiciary Committee conducts a full-scale investigation into the charges by gathering evidence and holding hearings in which witnesses for the "prosecution" and "defense" testify. Based on the evidence and testimony gathered during the investigation, the Judiciary Committee draws up articles of impeachment. These are formal charges of wrongdoing.

The articles of impeachment, along with the Judiciary Committee's recommendations, are then presented to the entire House of Representatives. House members study the committee's findings, debate the charges, and then vote on the articles. A simple majority vote in support of the articles results in their passage.

At this point, the official formally accused of wrongdoing by the House of Representatives is considered to be impeached. He or she is charged with a crime but has not yet been tried on those charges. The impeachment proceedings in the House are similar to a grand jury investigation, in which prosecutors introduce evidence of a suspect's involvement in a crime and a jury decides whether there is enough evidence to charge the defendant and send him or her to trial. If the jury votes yes, that suspect is indicted—or formally charged—and awaits trial. In the same way, a federal official who is formally accused of wrongdoing is impeached and moves to a trial in the U.S. Senate.

The Senate's Role

The Senate phase of the impeachment proceedings is indeed much like an ordinary trial, only with an extraordinary judge, jury, prosecution, and defendant. In cases of presidential impeachment, the chief justice of the Supreme Court presides over the trial. The "jury" of senators listens to House managers (representatives who

INTRODUCTION 11

Above is an illustration of the notice of Andrew Johnson's impeachment given by the House Judiciary Committee to the Senate. Johnson was the first American president to be impeached, though he was not convicted.

serve in the role of prosecuting attorneys); defense lawyers present evidence, call people to testify, and cross-examine witnesses.

After each side has presented its case, the Senate meets in private and deliberates on the charges and the evidence against the accused official. After thoroughly discussing and debating the case, the senators take a vote. Two-thirds of the 100 senators must vote "guilty" on any given article of impeachment for there to be a conviction on that particular charge. If the official is convicted on one or more articles of impeachment, he or she is automatically removed from office. The senators next vote on additional punishment, if any. In addition to removal, they can decide to prevent the official from ever holding a public office again. In the case of a president who is both impeached and convicted, the vice president immediately assumes the presidency.

A RARE BUT SOLEMN ACTION

A presidential impeachment is extremely uncommon, and there has never been a presidential conviction in American history. Although often threatened, impeachment itself is rare, and conviction on articles of impeachment is far rarer. Impeachment proceedings have been initiated against 62 federal officers since 1789, and only 17 of them have actually been impeached. This includes 2 presidents. Only 7 of the 17 were convicted on their articles of impeachment and removed from office, all of them judges.

In the end, the impeachment process is nothing more complicated than a grand jury investigation and trial, although one conducted by and among the highest levels of government and with the most profound of repercussions. Although all impeachment proceedings have followed the basic procedures mandated by the Constitution, each has offered its own unique political intrigue, legal wrangling, human drama, and historical curiosities. No two impeachments are alike, and the array of charges, criminal activities, vivid personalities, and hidden agendas they feature are rich and fascinating in their variety.

2

THE ORIGINS OF IMPEACHMENT

Despite the fact that the 13 original American colonies waged a long and violent revolution in order to free themselves from the oppressive interference of their mother country, England, many of the new nation's governmental structures, processes, and laws were inspired by English models.

The bicameral (two-chambered) Congress of the United States is modeled after the two-tiered English Parliament, which is composed of a lower House of Commons and an upper House of Lords. The two houses form the legislative branch of the English government. The American equivalents are the House of Representatives, which is the lower house, and the Senate, Congress's upper house. Similarly, England's "mixed" government of king or queen, nobles (lords), and commoners—a cross section of the population that in theory represents the interests of the entire society and creates a balance of power—is echoed in the three branches of the U.S. federal government. In the United States, the executive (president, vice president, and cabinet officials), legislative (Congress), and judicial (Supreme Court) branches of government check and balance each other's powers while providing for a representative democracy.

Even the U.S. Constitution—the founding document of the postrevolutionary nation and the blueprint for its new government—draws on England's thirteenth-century Magna Carta and seventeenth-century Bill of Rights for many of its lofty ideals and specific provisions. These include the right to jury trials, the right to bear arms, freedom from "cruel and unusual punishment," and prohibitions against unlawful arrest and imprisonment. Indeed, much of American common law (laws based on custom and precedent, or what has been judged in the past to be lawful or unlawful) is borrowed directly from the English legal system.

IMPEACHMENT IN MEDIEVAL ENGLAND

One of the constitutional provisions borrowed from the English political tradition is impeachment, a governmental tool that allows for the removal of judges, officials, and leaders who are corrupt or have committed some sort of crime related to their public offices.

In the early medieval period (before A.D. 1300), a primitive form of impeachment developed in England. In some of these impeachment cases, however, Parliament's role often seems to have been simply to ratify, or agree to, a judgment made by the king against an official or other subject. This may have served as a sort of "rubber stamp" that allowed the king to avoid creating the impression of tyrannical behavior by disguising his intentions as a governmentally reviewed and approved course of action.

Parliament Seizes Impeachment Power

It was not until 1376 that a Parliament-driven impeachment process would emerge in England. In that year, two English subjects were impeached by Parliament, one a noble and the other a commoner and London merchant. Both the noble, Lord William Latimer, and the commoner, Richard Lyons, were accused of misusing royal funds for personal interests. The important aspect of these two impeachments is that Parliament, rather than the king, initiated the proceedings. In fact, some historians believe that it is because the king, Edward III, showed so little interest in punishing Latimer and Lyons for their corruption that Parliament felt the need to step in and seize control of the impeachment process.

Parliament ordered the immediate arrest of Lyons and Latimer, but Latimer demanded that written charges be submitted first. He also insisted on time to review the charges and prepare a defense, followed by a proper trial before the House of Lords. Although formal written charges were never produced, Latimer did receive the time to prepare his defense, and he was tried before the upper house, as he had requested. In this way, the basic structure and proceedings of modern impeachment were established: Formal charges of wrongdoing are brought by the lower house, followed by a trial on those charges in the upper house, during which the lords serve as both judge and jury.

Perhaps realizing that it had developed a powerful new tool to influence the throne, Parliament began to treat impeachment as a way to check and curtail (reduce) royal power. Over time, Parliament came to approach impeachment as a means to try any peer (noble) or commoner for "high crimes and misdemeanors." This was a vague and wide-ranging spectrum of crimes that in practice included treason, bribery, misuse of public funds, incompetence in office, inappropriate or illegal influencing of the king's favor, corruption, oppression, drunkenness, and vulgarity.

The crimes themselves could often be a flimsy excuse to remove a minister who carried out unpopular royal policies. Because members of Parliament could not remove a king or queen whose policies they found objectionable, they instead removed the ministers who represented and enforced those policies. They often went after the highest royal officers, individuals who would otherwise be virtually untouchable by the ordinary laws and judicial system. Impeachment became Parliament's hedge against royal tyranny. In some measure, it made kings and queens accountable to a Parliament that could legally hinder their efforts and disrupt the royal administration.

Early on, in 1388, King Richard II recognized the danger to the throne that this new form of impeachment

THE ORIGINS OF IMPEACHMENT   17

England's King Richard II (1367–1400) is shown here on the throne. King Richard II recognized that the English Parliament's new form of impeachment was a danger to the throne, but was not able to take that power away from the Parliament.

represented. He challenged Parliament's right to launch impeachment proceedings without the king's consent. Several judges agreed with him and declared impeachment proceedings not sanctioned by the throne to be illegal. Parliament coolly responded by impeaching those judges and removing them from the bench. Parliament retained its exclusive right to impeach commoners, nobles, and royal officials; to try and convict them; and to determine appropriate punishments. Unlike the impeachment process that later developed in the United States, Parliament

WHAT CRIMES ARE CONSIDERED IMPEACHABLE?

What qualifies as an impeachable crime in the federal government of the United States has been shrouded in confusion and debate since the impeachment discussions of the Constitutional Convention. The nature of impeachable crimes—and the specific acts that would fall within the category—has become no clearer or more codified over time. Some people feel that an impeachable crime should be a crime that would be prosecuted in a criminal court if committed by an ordinary citizen. Others believe that impeachable crimes can include less serious misdeeds that are ethical and moral lapses although not necessarily criminal.

Treason and bribery are clearly specified by the Constitution as impeachable crimes. Treason is the betrayal of one's country and its interests, and bribery is the buying of influence or favors through cash or gifts. Precisely what is covered by the term "high crimes and misdemeanors," however, has been difficult to define and agree on. In his could issue criminal-style punishments for individuals convicted of impeachment charges, including jail time and even death by execution.

IMPEACHMENT AND PROTEST IN THE AMERICAN COLONIES

During the seventeenth century, in the period when England began to establish colonies in North America, parliamentary impeachment reached the height of its influence. Largely in response to the perceived excesses of the

book *Impeachment: The Constitutional Problems*, Raoul Berger cited then–House Representative Gerald Ford: "An impeachable offense is whatever a majority of the House considers it to be at a given moment in history." Ironically, only a few years later, Vice President Ford would become president of the United States after Richard Nixon's resignation under threat of presidential impeachment.

Past impeachment trials offer some guidance on the range of impeachable crimes and the specific misdeeds that qualify. Some of the crimes that federal officials have been impeached for include perjury (lying under oath), filing false income tax returns, obstruction of justice, extortion (a person forcing someone else to give him or her money or other things of value), abuse of power, interfering with elections, general misconduct, favoritism, conspiracy, fraud, filing false travel vouchers, improper use of private railroad cars, unlawful imprisonment, drunkenness, foul language, and insanity.

Stuart kings (James I, Charles I, Charles II, and James II), Parliament began to aggressively assert its right to impeachment and to attempt to influence policy by removing high-ranking royal representatives. This was a tense and violent period of political intrigue and civil war. Much of the anger and conflict were provoked by the monarchs' debt-spending, Catholic sympathies, court decadence (high living), corruption, and dictator-like style of rule.

Many of the early American colonists in the New World were opposed to Stuart policies, if not to the kings themselves, and they recognized the value of impeachment in fighting against corruption, tyranny, and harmful policies. As a result, colonial assemblies often claimed the right to impeach colonial officials, even though the Crown (the British monarch) never recognized such a right. As was the case in England, impeachment proceedings were mainly used to challenge the authority of officials who were otherwise unaccountable to the people.

Also as in England, a two-tiered system developed in which the actual trial was held by a higher council. The colonial assemblies had the power only to impeach (bring charges against) officials; they could not try them on those charges. Therefore, they had to call on governing councils or provincial councils to hear the charges, weigh the evidence, and decide the punishment upon conviction. In most cases, the colonists sought to remove officials, including royal governors, who either were guilty of poor governance or represented and enforced increasingly tyrannical colonial policies issued by the Crown or Parliament.

Colonial impeachment was mostly a symbolic exercise. It became more a form of protest against the Crown than a genuine mechanism for removal of colonial rulers. One royal governor, John Harvey of Virginia, was removed from office in 1635 as a result of impeachment proceedings. From 1700 to 1750, however, only four impeachments occurred in colonial assemblies, and none of them led to removal from office. Still, these opportunities to lodge formal protests against the policies and rule of the mother country created a precedent for legislative democracy and colonial self-assertion that would inspire and embolden far more widespread and consequential acts of resistance in the years that led up to the American Revolution.

Indeed, the contents of the Declaration of Independence can be viewed as articles of impeachment brought by the 13 colonies against the largest empire in the world. The "trial" would be a long, bloody, destructive war; the outcome would be decided in the complainants' favor; and the punishment would be England's loss of the colonies. The United States was born.

3

The Creation of a Federal Impeachment Process

By the time the colonies declared their independence from England and became the United States of America, they had become familiar and comfortable with the impeachment process and recognized its importance as a tool to curb the corruptions of power. More than half of the 13 original states included impeachment provisions in their constitutions. The specific formulation of the impeachment process varied from state to state, with the greatest differences arising from the question of what constituted an impeachable crime.

The process was occasionally abused. For example, sometimes private citizens who had remained loyal to the Crown during the Revolution were punished by being impeached and having their land and property seized. In general, however, the states decided to narrow the focus of impeachment to target only public officials currently serving in office who were accused of crimes committed in office that related to their public duties. Punishments were limited to removal from office and the forbidding of future office holding. This was a major divergence from the English model, in which Parliament could impeach any member of the realm, including a private citizen, for any crime whatsoever, and impose criminal penalties including fines, imprisonment, and execution.

Some states adopted a very narrow definition of impeachable crimes. Pennsylvania's constitution stated that a public official could be impeached only for "maladministration," or incompetent governance. This meant that any crime committed that was unrelated to the official's office and its duties—such as public drunkenness, theft (if the theft was not of public funds or property), or murder—would have to be tried in the ordinary court system. New York and North Carolina added corruption to maladministration when they composed their lists of impeachable offenses. As quoted in Matthew Romney's article "The Origins and Scope of Presidential Impeachment," to maladministration and corruption Delaware added a rather vague and open-ended warning that anything "by which the safety of the commonwealth may be endangered" would be considered an impeachable crime. New Jersey went even further in keeping its impeachment options open by listing simple but unspecified "misbehavior" as grounds for impeachment.

Where state impeachment trials would be held and by whom also differed from state to state. Most states duplicated the English model and held the trials in their upper houses. Sometimes state judges presided over the proceedings. In Virginia, impeachments were tried by the state Supreme Court.

THE CONSTITUTIONAL CONVENTION

In the summer of 1787, delegates from the 13 original states gathered in Philadelphia, Pennsylvania, to hold the Constitutional Convention. They were charged with adopting a new plan of government that would shore up the weaknesses that had become apparent in the Articles of Confederation, the new nation's first constitution.

At the time of the drafting of the Articles of Confederation, in the midst of war with England and in the wake of the former colonies' recent harsh experiences with the mother country's tyranny, most Revolutionary-era Americans had been wary of creating a strong federal government. They feared its potential to interfere with state and local matters, become oppressive and dictatorial, and demand taxes of the sort that had provoked so much conflict with the English Parliament before the Revolution.

A FEDERAL IMPEACHMENT PROCESS 25

In the summer of 1787, delegates from the 13 original states gathered in Philadelphia for what would become known as the Constitutional Convention. In this illustration, George Washington stands on the dais at the signing of the Constitution.

As a result, the drafters of the Articles of Confederation provided for a weak central government that had no executive branch (no president) and could not raise taxes, enforce its own laws, regulate domestic and international trade and commerce, or negotiate with foreign powers.

Because the drafters of the Constitution largely agreed on the need for a stronger federal government, including the creation of an executive branch, the issue of impeachment—the ability to charge, convict, and remove the executive if necessary—became important in Constitutional Convention debates. Although intent on strengthening the central government, many Americans and convention delegates were still nervous about placing too much power in one person's hands. If it was necessary to create a presidency for the smooth functioning and growth of the United States, it was equally necessary to create a mechanism for that official's removal should he or she become corrupted by power or prove to be incompetent. The American people and their delegates did not feel comfortable with the idea of electing a president if they were not also assured that, in grave circumstances, they could oust him or her from office between elections.

IMPEACHMENT DEBATES

Agreeing on and drafting the Constitution's provisions for impeachment would be no simple task, however. Because state practices varied so much, there was no one model to draw on or duplicate. Disagreements quickly arose over several important issues. The most important of these were the proper "court" for the impeachment trial (the Senate, Supreme Court, or a council of state governors); the impeachability of the president (not all delegates felt that removal of the executive any way besides an election was wise); which offenses would be considered impeachable; and how many votes would be required to convict an official on impeachment charges (a simple majority or some greater number).

The Constitutional Convention delegates who took a particular interest in formulating the federal impeachment process included some of the brightest lights of Revolutionary-era America, such as Benjamin Franklin, James Madison, and Alexander Hamilton. Most of them came from states with well-established impeachment procedures, with which they were very familiar. As a result, a few common and popular elements based on state models were agreed on immediately. For example, it was quickly decided that only public officials, not private citizens, could be impeached. These officials could be impeached only for crimes committed in office, rather than for misdeeds that may have occurred in private life. Finally, the only punishment that would result from the American version of impeachment would be removal from office and the possible barring of future office holding. No criminal penalties, such as jail time, could be ordered by the body that judged impeachment charges, and the death penalty was certainly out of the question.

Where Would Trials Occur and Who Would Conduct Them?

After this early flush of agreement and harmony, however, the delegates soon became bogged down in disagreement over how to structure the impeachment process. The first major debate centered on which government body would have the power to try officials on charges of impeachment. It was widely agreed that impeachment charges would be made in the House of Representatives, the lower house of the U.S. Congress. There was much less agreement over where the trial would occur and who would conduct it once the charges were filed.

In the early days of the convention, Edmund Randolph of Virginia introduced his proposed plan for the nation's new Constitution. This became known as the Virginia Plan. In it, Randolph called for the creation of a national judiciary (like today's Supreme Court) that, among other things, would have the power to impeach "national officers." James Madison agreed with Randolph, but William Paterson, the attorney general of New Jersey, proposed an alternative constitutional plan, known as the New Jersey Plan. Unhappy with the absence of a congressional role in impeachment in the Virginia Plan, Paterson's plan allowed for a national judiciary to impeach and try public officials, yet only Congress would be granted the exclusive power to remove the chief executive if requested by a majority of state governors. Congress would not have the right to impeach or try cases, however.

At this point, Alexander Hamilton weighed in. He proposed that a court of state chief judges (one from each state) should preside over all impeachment trials. The "governor" (chief executive or president), senators, and other officers of the federal government (including judges) could be impeached for "maladministration" and "corrupt conduct." If convicted, they would be removed and barred from future public office.

A compromise proposal was then issued, calling for the House of Representatives to be granted the sole power of impeachment, with the Supreme Court presiding over the trial phase of the proceedings. This idea caused concern, however, because some delegates feared that, since Supreme Court justices would be appointed by the president, they would be reluctant to turn around and convict that

A FEDERAL IMPEACHMENT PROCESS   29

The first president of the United States, George Washington *(left)*, also formed the first presidential cabinet. For his cabinet, Washington chose some of the most influential men of the time *(from right to left)*: Edmund Jennings Randolph, Thomas Jefferson, Alexander Hamilton, and Henry Knox.

person in an impeachment trial. In addition, if the official's impeachable offense was also a criminal offense, he or she might face two trials—an impeachment trial and a criminal trial—presided over by the same judges. The fear was that judges would be less fair-minded and objective in a criminal trial if they had already convicted the individual in an impeachment trial on the same or related charges.

Finally, a special committee strongly urged the convention delegates to accept a proposal that granted the Senate—the upper house of Congress—the power to try all impeachment cases. Earlier in the Constitutional Convention, it was proposed that the president be appointed by the Senate. Some people therefore feared that the Senate would become far too powerful if it had the ability to both appoint and remove the nation's chief executive. The president would in effect become a puppet of the Senate, forced to do its will or face removal. Eventually, however, the convention decided that the president would be selected by the Electoral College (a group of representatives from each state who vote for a presidential candidate based on the popular vote of their states' citizens), not by the Senate. This removed most objections to Senate impeachment trials.

Could the President Be Impeachable?

The second important subject of debate regarding impeachment was the issue of whether the president would be subject to the process at all. Again, some delegates were concerned that, if a president could be removed, he or she would be too dependent on Congress and have to spend too much effort keeping House and Senate members happy. Others believed that the possibility of serving more than one presidential term and having to run for reelection would force the president to behave properly in office. If he or she didn't, the election itself would serve as a kind of impeachment process. Still others felt that limiting the president to a single term in office would eliminate the need for an impeachment process.

The majority opinion, however, was that impeachment was a necessary check on the executive, who might otherwise become oppressive or corrupt without penalty. In his book *Presidential Impeachment*, John R. Labovitz quoted George Mason, a delegate from Virginia, as stating, "No point is of more importance than that the right of impeachment should be continued. Shall any man be above Justice? Above all, shall that man be above it, who can commit the most extensive injustice?"

According to Labovitz's book *Presidential Impeachment*, James Madison agreed, believing it

> *indispensable that some provision should be made for defending the Community [against] the incapacity, negligence, or perfidy of the chief Magistrate.... He might lose his capacity after his appointment. He might pervert his administration into a scheme of peculation [embezzlement, or theft of funds] or oppression. He might betray his trust to foreign powers.*

Because this kind of presidential incompetence and corruption could be "fatal to the Republic," Madison strongly argued for the power of executive impeachment.

Massachusetts delegate Elbridge Gerry also insisted on the necessity of the impeachment process, claiming that there was no danger or downside associated with the process. It would simply be irrelevant to good and honest presidents and a healthy caution to potentially dishonest and corruptible ones. Benjamin Franklin even claimed that presidential impeachment was necessary because the only other way to remove a leader who had become "obnoxious" would be assassination. He pointed out that impeachment would also offer the president the chance to "vindicate his character," an opportunity he would not otherwise have.

Fresh from the upheaval of revolution and run-ins with an untouchable king, many delegates worried that, without impeachment, the nation would be torn by violent revolt every time a president abused the power of the office. Ultimately, the convention delegates decided

IMPEACHMENT PROVISIONS IN THE U.S. CONSTITUTION

The following are the relevant sections of the U.S. Constitution that provide for a federal impeachment process:

Article 1, Section 2, Clause 5 The House of Representatives shall choose their Speaker and other Officers; and shall have the sole Power of Impeachment.

Article 1, Section 3, Clause 6 The Senate shall have the sole Power to try all Impeachments. When sitting for that Purpose, they shall be on Oath or Affirmation. When the President of the United States is tried, the Chief Justice shall preside: And no Person shall be convicted without the Concurrence of two thirds of the Members present.

Article 1, Section 3, Clause 7 Judgment in Cases of Impeachment shall not extend further than to removal

A FEDERAL IMPEACHMENT PROCESS

that the president could be impeached and removed for "malpractice or neglect of duty."

What Offenses Would Be Considered Impeachable?

These grounds for removal of the president led to the next major source of debate concerning impeachment, one that would continue to flare up long after the Constitution was drafted, signed, and ratified: What offenses would be considered impeachable? Some delegates felt that the

from Office, and disqualification to hold and enjoy any Office of honor, Trust or Profit under the United States: but the Party convicted shall nevertheless be liable and subject to Indictment, Trial, Judgment and Punishment, according to Law.

Article 2, Section 2, Clause 1 The President shall ... have Power to grant Reprieves and Pardons for Offenses against the United States, except in Cases of Impeachment.

Article 2, Section 4, Clause 1 The President, Vice President and all civil Officers of the United States, shall be removed from Office on Impeachment for, and Conviction of, Treason, Bribery, or other high Crimes and Misdemeanors.

offenses should be limited to misbehavior that related directly to their official duties. These included "maladministration," corruption, neglect of duty, and misconduct. Others felt that, in addition to these "offenses in office," some common-law crimes, such as murder and treason (betrayal of one's country), should also provide grounds for impeachment.

A special committee proposed to resolve the dispute by listing only treason and bribery as grounds for presidential impeachment. Some delegates objected that a wide range of official crimes and violations of the Constitution would not be covered by these two offenses, however, and it was then proposed that "maladministration" be added to the list to allow for the punishment of a wider range of offenses.

This, too, provoked disagreement, with James Madison objecting to the use of such a broad, vague term. It was feared that "maladministration" would serve as a grab bag of possible charges, allowing Congress to charge and remove a president with whom it was displeased but who had done nothing truly criminal or corrupt. Others agreed with Madison, and the wording that was approved was "treason, bribery, or other high crimes and misdemeanors against the United States."

In many respects, however, this formulation of impeachable offenses is no less vague than "maladministration," and nearly every generation since has grappled with exactly what sorts of official crimes and public misbehavior fit under that big umbrella.

A FEDERAL IMPEACHMENT PROCESS

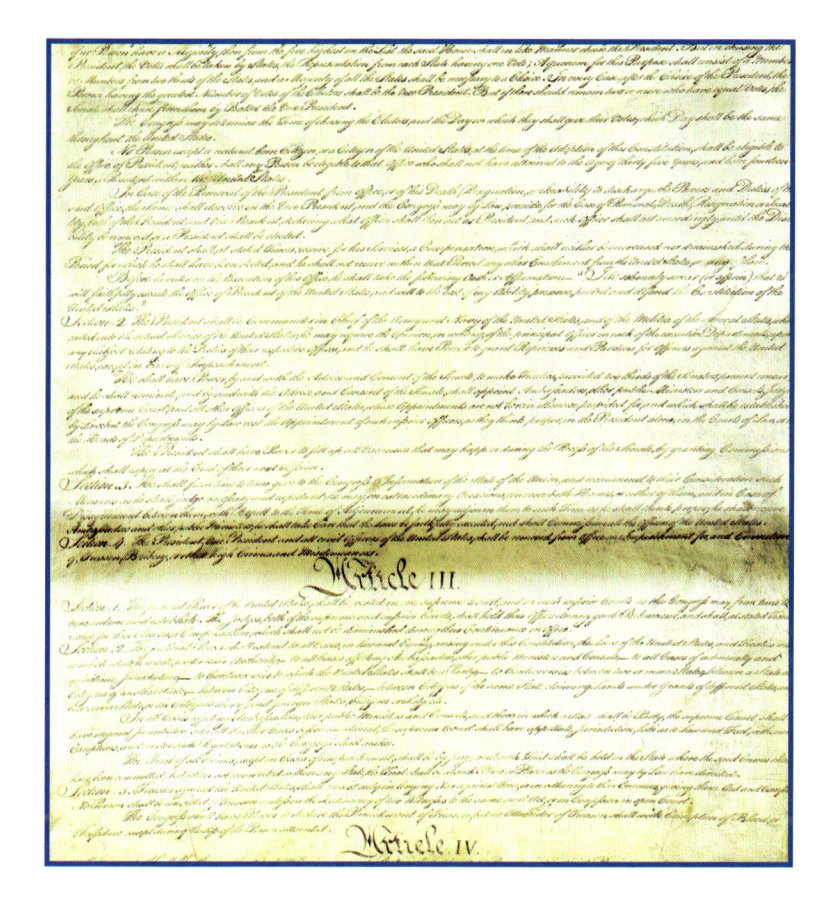

A page from the Constitution is shown here. The highlighted portion shows the article governing impeachment, which reads as follows: "The President, Vice President and all civil officers of the United States, shall be removed from office on impeachment for, and conviction of, treason, bribery, or other high crimes and misdemeanors."

How Many Votes Would Be Required to Convict?

The final thorny issue to resolve was how many votes in the Senate would be required to convict and remove a president. During the Constitutional Convention, it gradually became accepted that issues of great importance—such as ratification of treaties, passage of congressional acts, and confirmation of important nominations to offices and judgeships—should require a "supermajority" rather than a "simple majority." In these cases, a supermajority meant a vote in favor by two-thirds of the Senate (rather than just more than half). Obtaining a supermajority on any decision would require an extra amount of care, debate, and consideration, ensuring that crucial decisions were given all the time and thought that they required to be made properly.

The requirement of a supermajority vote to convict also helped guarantee that a leader would not be removed hastily, in the heat of a political moment. If the charges were politically motivated or part of a personal or party grudge rather than true offenses that harmed the office and the nation, it would be less likely that two-thirds of the senators would in good conscience be able to vote for conviction.

With relatively little debate, the delegates recognized the importance of requiring a supermajority to convict and remove any high public official, the president in particular. The final piece of the impeachment process was now in place. Thus, in the course of the Constitutional Convention, the delegates had decided that public officials, including the president, could be impeached (for a vague mix of criminal offenses and official misconduct) by the House and tried in the Senate. If a two-thirds vote for conviction was achieved, that official would be removed from office and prevented from ever serving in government again. The new nation had crafted its impeachment process. How well it would work was something that none of the delegates looked forward to testing.

4

Impeachment Proceedings in the House of Representatives

The main impeachment provisions that appear in the U.S. Constitution amount to only half a dozen small articles that, taken together, provide a barebones indication of how the impeachment process should be structured and carried out. It fell to the representatives and senators of the late eighteenth and early nineteenth centuries to interpret and flesh out the Constitution's skeletal framework for impeachment by trying actual cases. The impeachment process in place today is the product of trial and error and tinkering since the Constitution went into effect more than 200 years ago.

When a president, vice president, federal judge, cabinet member, or other "civil officer of the United States" is suspected of "treason, bribery, or other high crimes and misdemeanors," how and by whom is the impeachment process triggered? Once triggered, how and where does the process unfold? Who are the major players?

ACCUSATION AND INVESTIGATION

The impeachment process begins quite simply, with only two individuals: the person who is suspected of wrongdoing and the person who complains about it. An official complaint of misconduct in office must be filed with the House of Representatives in order to get the ball rolling. This complaint can be filed by almost anyone, including a private citizen. Ordinarily, however, the complaint is made by a House representative, a state legislature, a grand jury, a special prosecutor, a federal judicial conference, or the president (in cases in which charges against judges or other nonpresidential officials are being sought).

Having received the official complaint of misconduct, the House of Representatives must begin to grapple with the accusation and determine its merit. The immediate first step is to pass the complaint to the House's Judiciary Committee, which, among other things, has jurisdiction over the federal judiciary (courts and judges), criminal law enforcement, and administrative procedure. The complaint is then usually forwarded to one of the Judiciary

House Judiciary Committee Chairman Henry Hyde (R-Ill.), center, presides over a committee hearing on October 5, 1998, to discuss whether to open an impeachment inquiry against President Bill Clinton.

Committee's subcommittees. A lawyer for each party (Republican and Democrat) reviews the charges, and they make a report within two weeks. If more information is needed (it almost always is), the subcommittee is given the authority to launch an investigation of the complaint and to begin to gather evidence, if any, of the misconduct of which the official is accused.

In some cases, a criminal trial on the same or similar charges contained in the complaint will already have been conducted. This makes the Judiciary Committee's investigation much easier, because records of the trial proceedings contain much of the evidence that would have to have been gathered by the House. The danger of a criminal trial occurring before an impeachment proceeding is that the trial's outcome—conviction or acquittal—may influence the opinions of the House members who are either evaluating the validity of the official complaint or voting on whether to impeach the accused official. They may not be as objective in their decision making as they would be if that official had not already been judged in a criminal court.

Whether gathering information in a fresh investigation or collecting and reviewing material from an earlier criminal trial, the Judiciary Committee must review a large amount of evidence in order to determine whether it will recommend formally charging the official. This evidence can be gathered from many sources: committee investigations, materials from grand jury hearings and criminal trials, subpoenaed (officially requested and required) documents, and live testimony before the committee.

ARTICLES OF IMPEACHMENT

If the evidence gathered during the investigation by the Judiciary Committee is strong enough to support charges of impeachable misconduct—if at least one impeachable offense seems to have occurred—the committee drafts one or more articles of impeachment. These are formal charges of wrongdoing. It also writes a report of findings, stating its recommendation to the House to adopt the articles of impeachment against the official in question. If no compelling evidence is gathered or if there is evidence of wrongdoing but the offense is not considered impeachable misconduct, the committee reports these findings to the House and the impeachment process stops immediately.

On receiving the articles of impeachment and the Judiciary Committee's recommendation, the full House may revise the articles somewhat, possibly dropping one or more of the charges. It can even add articles of impeachment not drafted and recommended by the committee, although this is very unlikely. In general, the House respects the investigation and judgment of the Judiciary Committee and follows its recommendations carefully. Debate on the articles follows, but new evidence is rarely brought forth.

VOTING TO IMPEACH

After some debate, the House must vote on whether to impeach—formally accuse and charge—the official. A vote to impeach requires only a simple majority of representatives present (50 percent plus one). The vote may be on all of the articles of impeachment at once, or each article may be voted on individually.

A majority vote in favor of the articles means that the accused official has now formally been impeached. He or she has been formally charged with misconduct (usually of a criminal nature) and now awaits trial in the Senate.

HOUSE MANAGERS

The final step in the House before the impeachment process shifts to the Senate is the appointment of House "managers." Managers are House representatives who

IMPEACHMENT PROCEEDINGS IN THE HOUSE

On December 19, 1998, the House of Representatives voted to impeach President Bill Clinton. Above, Clinton shakes hands with supporters just after the announcement was made.

are chosen to "prosecute" or argue the case against the impeached official in the Senate. They serve as the equivalent of prosecuting attorneys. Managers are usually drawn from both political parties to avoid the appearance of a politically motivated attack on the impeached official. Managers also are chosen from the ranks of representatives who had voted in favor of impeachment. There would be no point in selecting a manager to argue the case for impeachment if he or she had not believed that there were grounds for impeachment in the first place.

The House managers orally impeach (or accuse) the official in the Senate chamber, reading out the articles of impeachment. The proceedings have now shifted to the upper house of Congress, where senators serve as jurors, sitting in judgment of the impeached public official. The chairperson of the House managers then requests that the Senate order the impeached official to respond to the charges contained in the articles of impeachment. The chairperson also requests a conviction on the charges and the resulting punishment. The managers then oversee and actively prosecute the official in the upper house. The trial phase of the impeachment process has begun.

5

Impeachment Proceedings in the Senate

The Constitution states that the House of Representatives has the "sole power of impeachment"—the exclusive right to formally accuse a public official of misconduct and wrongdoing in office. Likewise, the Constitution declares that the Senate has the "sole power to try all impeachments." The Senate is the government body that must accept the awesome responsibility of deciding a public official's guilt or innocence and possible banishment from public life. This grave burden becomes even heavier when the public official in question is the president of the United States.

Having received the articles of impeachment from the House managers, the Senate transforms itself into a trial jury of sorts. Each senator takes a special oath, swearing to administer justice according to the Constitution and federal laws. It may decide at the outset to revise the rules of impeachment trials, usually in response to some part of the process that proved to be flawed in previous impeachment proceedings. Any vote to change rules and procedures requires a simple majority in favor.

TRIAL PROCEDURES

In cases of presidential impeachment, the chief justice of the Supreme Court presides over the proceedings as a sort of trial judge. He or she oversees the process and rules on all procedural questions, including what evidence can and cannot be presented in presidential trials. The chief justice's rulings, however, can be overturned by the senators with a simple majority vote. The senators remain silent during the trial, although they submit written questions for witnesses to the chief justice. In presidential impeachments, the president can appear to testify on his or her own behalf, but he or she can also request to be absent (a request that would probably be granted by the Senate). If the president is absent, his or her lawyers handle the entire defense.

The impeachment trial can be conducted in one of two ways. Traditionally, the trial would be conducted before the full Senate. The senators would weigh the case by listening to the evidence presented by both the House managers and the defendant's lawyers. In nonpresidential

IMPEACHMENT PROCEEDINGS IN THE SENATE

In cases of presidential impeachment, the chief justice of the U.S. Supreme Court presides over the proceedings in the Senate. Above, Chief Justice William Rehnquist is sworn in for the impeachment trial of President Clinton in 1998.

impeachment trials, the Senate would also hear and decide arguments concerning what evidence should and should not be allowed to be presented and which trial proceedings were or were not constitutional.

In recent decades, a second trial format has been more frequently used. In part because senators were often criticized for being absent during impeachment trials, new rules were established that allowed the Senate to create a special committee of 12 senators (similar to a regular criminal jury) to hear the evidence and testimony. This also addressed the issue of senators who frequently complained about how complicated and time consuming impeachment trial proceedings were.

Some critics feel that this is an unconstitutional revision of the process outlined in the Constitution because the document's framers clearly state that "the Senate" has sole power to try impeachments, not some small segment of the Senate. In any case, a special committee would probably never be used to try a presidential impeachment case because of the trial's grave importance to the government and the nation. Senators would not want to risk seeming too casual or unconcerned by not fully and carefully participating in the trial of their president.

The Senate committee acts just as the full Senate would, gathering evidence, hearing testimony, and ruling on motions (or requests) put forth by the House managers or defense counsel. After receiving the evidence that relates to the misconduct of the official and hearing the defense's counterarguments, the committee writes up a transcript of the testimony it has heard (a word-for-word account of everything that has been said). It presents this to the full Senate along with a statement of the undisputed facts of the case and a summary of the evidence that relates to the aspects of the case that are disputed by the House managers and the impeached official's lawyers. In recent decades, the Senate committee's proceedings and all testimony have also been videotaped. When the case returns to the full Senate, senators can view these if they wish to help them gain more information and make up their minds about the official's guilt or innocence.

The committee provides all of this material—the transcript, the statement of facts, the summary of evidence, and the videotaped proceedings—to the full Senate without stating an opinion on guilt or innocence or making any recommendation about how the Senate should vote.

DEBATE AND DELIBERATIONS

The full Senate then pores over all of the evidence and testimony it has been given. After reviewing the material, the senators meet and discuss how satisfied they are with the quality and relevance of the testimony. If they feel that anything is lacking, they can call witnesses to testify before them or have evidence resubmitted. Once satisfied that the evidence is reasonably complete and that a suitably clear, detailed, and accurate picture of the case has emerged, the senators listen to the closing arguments of the House managers and the defendant's lawyers. This is the last chance for both sides to summarize their cases and persuade the senators of the truth of their positions.

Having been given the case, the senators now must debate among themselves the evidence that they have received and whether it points to the guilt or innocence of the impeached official. These debates are never public. Unlike some impeachment proceedings, they cannot be televised, reporters are not present, transcripts are not kept, and members of the public cannot sit in attendance. At this point, members of the special Senate impeachment committee can finally express their opinions about the defendant's guilt or innocence and recommend how to vote.

VOTING TO CONVICT

After a complete and thorough debate, the senators are ready to vote on one of the most momentous matters that they are likely to face during their terms in office. A separate vote is held on each of the articles of impeachment before them. A two-thirds vote in favor of conviction on any one of the articles results in the official's conviction and immediate removal from office. The Senate can then choose to hold a separate vote on whether to bar the impeached and convicted official from ever holding public office in the future. This further punishment requires a simple majority vote (although some constitutional scholars feel that this vote, like the one for conviction and removal, should require a supermajority). This extra punishment is simply an option; the Senate does not have to pursue it if it feels that conviction and removal from office are punishment enough.

If the Senate delivers a guilty verdict on a president, the chief justice of the Supreme Court will then rise and officially pronounce the president's conviction and removal from office. Once a president is impeached, convicted, and removed, the vice president immediately assumes the presidency.

An official convicted on articles of impeachment cannot be pardoned by the president, and convicted presidents cannot be pardoned by future presidents. A conviction in the Senate also does not shield the official from the filing of criminal charges. An impeachment trial does not take the place of a criminal trial; it is only meant to remove the wrongdoer and prevent him or her from committing further crimes while in office. It is up to the judicial system to try the official on the charges that

POOR ATTENDANCE RECORD

One consistent criticism of the impeachment process throughout its history has been the poor attendance and occasionally casual attitude of senators during the trial phase. The Constitution does not require a senator to attend all of the trial or even to be present for important votes, but widespread and frequent absences create a bad impression and can shake the public's faith in the fairness and integrity of the process.

Occasionally, more diligent representatives and senators express shock and disgust with the laxness of their colleagues. Michael J. Gerhardt quoted an official in his book *The Federal Impeachment Process*: During the 1913 impeachment trial of Circuit Court Judge Robert Archbald (impeached for, among other things, corruption, bribery, and extortion), it was observed that "the trial rarely attracted the attention of more than twenty senators. . . . [T]he senators, far from behaving like judges and jurors during a trial, wandered in and out of the Senate chamber at will."

The U.S. Senate Web article on impeachment offers another example: During the 1933 impeachment trial of District Court Judge Harold Louderback on charges of favoritism and conspiracy, Representative and House Manager Hatton Sumners of Texas took a dim view of his Senate counterparts: "At one time only three senators were present, and for ten days we presented evidence to what was practically an empty chamber."

relate to his or her criminal acts and assign the appropriate criminal punishment.

If no article of impeachment receives a two-thirds vote for conviction, the official is immediately declared to be acquitted (cleared of the charges). An acquitted president informs the Senate president and House speaker in writing of his or her ability to again "discharge their powers and duties of office." Acquittal is not the same thing as a declaration of innocence, however. The failed vote for conviction may reflect a lack of convincing, compelling evidence rather than a genuine belief that the official is innocent and was wrongfully accused. In general, any official who is impeached is often tainted by a lingering suspicion of guilt, even if he or she is ultimately acquitted.

THE POSSIBILITY OF APPEAL

Some constitutional scholars believe that there is still one last avenue open to a public official who has been impeached and convicted: the Supreme Court. They claim that nothing in the constitutional provisions for impeachment prevents an official from appealing his or her conviction to the Supreme Court and having it overturned and the office restored.

This path has only been tried once, and it failed. In 1989, U.S. District Judge Walter L. Nixon Jr. of Mississippi was convicted by the Senate of perjury (lying under oath) and removed from the bench. In 1993, he brought his case to the Supreme Court. The justices refused to hear his appeal, however, saying that they had no power to hear appeals of impeachment convictions. Because the Constitution clearly grants the Senate the "sole power" to try impeachments, a majority of justices on the Supreme Court did not feel that any other institution could pass judgment on the Senate's decision.

6

Notable Impeachment Proceedings in U.S. History

Despite the earnest and passionate debate about the need for impeachment by the framers of the Constitution and despite the elaborate accusation and trial processes that have sprung up from the rudimentary impeachment provisions found in that document, this powerful tool for enforcing good behavior among the highest judicial and executive officials has rarely been used.

The House of Representatives has launched impeachment proceedings only 62 times in more than 215 years.

Only 17 of these cases have resulted in impeachment, including 2 presidents, Andrew Johnson and Bill Clinton. Also in this group were 13 federal judges, 1 cabinet member, and 1 senator. Seven of these impeachments have resulted in conviction and removal from office, all of them judges. Of the remaining 10 cases, 7 resulted in acquittals (including both presidents), 1 was dismissed by the Senate, and 2 ended when the defendants resigned their judgeships.

Although rare, the impeachment proceedings and trials that have taken place were, in their own ways, fascinating dramas and riveting political theater. Each impeachment trial has interpreted constitutional provisions slightly differently, helping to clarify, for example, the powers of Congress, the nature of impeachable offenses, and the types of officials who could be considered impeachable.

SENATOR WILLIAM BLOUNT

The first federal impeachment to occur in the United States was also destined to be the last of its kind. The impeachment of Tennessee Senator William Blount in 1797 would be the first and last time a U.S. representative or senator would be subject to the impeachment process. Blount's trial helped clarify exactly which public officials were and were not impeachable.

Unauthorized Intrigue and Meddling

Blount ran afoul of Congress by unlawfully meddling in international and Native American political affairs. In the late eighteenth century, the Louisiana and Florida territories were not yet American possessions. They were controlled by Spain, but Great Britain was trying to seize them. The United States maintained a position of neutrality in this conflict, but Blount secretly entered into an effort to encourage the area's Cherokee and Creek tribes to launch a military expedition against the Spanish territories. The conquered lands would then be handed over to the British.

When information regarding this secret plot leaked out, there was great fear that Blount's meddling could embroil the still-young and politically immature nation in an international incident for which it was ill prepared. Massachusetts Representative John Adams initiated impeachment proceedings against Blount. On July 7, 1797, the House voted to impeach the senator, and the very next day the Senate voted 25 to 1 to expel him.

As quoted in Raoul Berger's book *Impeachment: The Constitutional Problems,* the stated reason for the expulsion was that Blount was "guilty of a high misdemeanor entirely inconsistent with his public trust and duty as a senator." Without official approval, Blount had involved the country in an international war, and this act came dangerously close to treason (the betrayal of one's country and its interests). The Senate expulsion was not a vote on the articles of impeachment but rather an immediate removal action taken independently of the impeachment process. The Senate still intended to hold an impeachment trial, even after its removal of the senator.

Blount's Successful Defense

Blount responded by arguing that, because he had been kicked out of the Senate, the upper chamber no longer had any jurisdiction, or legal authority, over him. It no longer had the right or power to try him on articles of impeachment. In addition, he claimed that the alleged crime was committed by him in a private capacity, not through his office. He was acting on Great Britain's behalf not as a senator but as a private citizen.

Furthermore, he argued that, even if he had not already been expelled, he could not be impeached because representatives and senators are not "civil officers" of the United States. The Constitution specifies that only the president, vice president, and civil officers of the United States are impeachable. Blount claimed that civil officers were those figures who are appointed by the president, such as federal judges and cabinet members, not democratically elected officials.

This last point turned out to be a crafty and persuasive argument, one that may have appealed to Blount's former congressional colleagues, who no doubt also wanted to be free of the threat of impeachment. On January 10, 1798, the Senate voted 14 to 11 to reject a resolution that would declare Blount a civil officer of the United States. A vote in favor would have cleared the way for the ex-senator's impeachment. A year later, on January 14, 1799, the Senate voted by the exact same margin to dismiss Blount's case, saying that the Senate had no jurisdiction in the matter.

Since that day, both the House and the Senate have operated on the understanding that their members are not impeachable. There has not been a single impeachment proceeding initiated against a representative or senator since the dismissal of Blount's case. Instead, Congress has various means to police and punish its members, including censure (a formal, public reprimand) and expulsion; however, Congress has no power to bar an expelled member from again serving as a representative or senator in the future. If that person can get elected again, he or she can reenter the halls of Congress.

JUDGE JOHN PICKERING

A few years after the dismissal of Senator William Blount's impeachment case, the first federal impeachment proceedings to result in a conviction occurred in strange and dramatic fashion. The official in question was New Hampshire U.S. District Court Judge John Pickering. Unlike the "high misdemeanors" and grave governmental crimes committed by Blount, Judge Pickering's crimes were of a more personal nature, although they proved to be entirely disruptive of his public duties.

Drunkenness, Blasphemy, and Insanity

The impeachment arose from a specific court case that he presided over, although the erratic behavior at the center of the impeachment charges had probably become typical of his actions on the bench during this time. In a case concerning shipping duties (fees and taxes) due to the

United States, Judge Pickering was accused of errors in judgment and procedure that hurt the country's interests. He was also said to have been drunk and using foul language while presiding over this flawed case.

The poorly judged case and Pickering's odd behavior during it were brought to the attention of the House of Representatives, which in 1803 voted to impeach him by a vote of 45 to 8. The articles of impeachment charged him with profanity and drunkenness on the bench and judicial decisions that seemed unrelated to the facts of the cases or the relevant laws.

ESCAPE THROUGH RESIGNATION

Some public officials attempt to dodge the humiliation of impeachment and the resulting trial by resigning from office before the articles of impeachment can be voted on. President Richard M. Nixon provides probably the most famous example of this strategy. In general, it is a highly effective tactic. The House of Representatives almost never pursues an impeachment inquiry after a suspected official's resignation—although there is no constitutional barrier to impeaching former officeholders for crimes committed while in office. In fact, most of the delegates to the Constitutional Convention assumed that the best time to impeach the president would be after he or she left office. Only gradually did a debate emerge over whether or not the president would be impeachable while still in office.

Judge Pickering was so unwell that he could not be present to defend himself in the Senate. Instead, his son arrived to plead with the Senators to postpone the trial, saying that his father was insane, incapable of good judgment, and unable to perform his duties and therefore should not be tried for misconduct that was beyond his control. The Senate was unmoved, however, and insisted that the trial proceed, even though there would be no defense.

Where Was the Crime?

It was apparent that the judge, although undeniably mentally ill and no longer capable of performing his job, had not committed any "high crime or misdemeanor." Drunkenness and bad language were not federal crimes, nor was insanity. Even his misinterpretation of the law could not be considered a crime. He may have demonstrated errors in judgment, but no one was accusing him of corruption or intentional violation of the law. For this reason, the Senate did not vote on each article of impeachment but instead voted to declare Pickering "guilty as charged." This gave the senators a way to avoid voting on whether the crimes he was accused of committing were truly impeachable offenses. In fact, 5 senators removed themselves from the trial and abstained from voting in protest of what they considered to be "procedural irregularities." Nevertheless, the remaining senators voted 19 to 7 to convict Pickering and 20 to 6 to remove him from office.

Like the 5 senators who protested the vote on Pickering's articles of impeachment, many modern scholars and observers are troubled by the precedent set by this case.

They feel that, by impeaching and convicting Judge Pickering for drunkenness, bad language, and insanity, the vague term "high crimes and misdemeanors" was made even more of a catchall category. The Pickering case, they argue, opened the door to impeachments based on noncriminal charges. Among other things, such a development made it far more likely that impeachment could become a highly politicized process. One party could potentially target the leading officers of a rival party without being required to prove that serious crimes were committed in office and against the interests of the nation and its people.

Along these lines, it should be noted that Pickering was a member of the Federalist Party. The 19 senators who voted for his conviction were Republicans; the 7 who voted to acquit were Federalists.

JUSTICE SAMUEL CHASE

The very next federal impeachment to occur after the Senate trial of Judge Pickering heightened the sense that impeachment was becoming a dangerously politicized tool, a means to check the power of a rival political party. Soon after Pickering's conviction, a second Federalist judge, Samuel Chase, associate justice of the U.S. Supreme Court, was impeached by the House of Representatives.

Intemperate, Inflammatory, and Indecent

The charges arose out of four cases that Chase tried between 1800 and 1803 as a circuit court judge. Among other things, he was accused of issuing improper instructions to the jury, consistent bias against the defense and defendants, abusing and ridiculing the defense, excluding testimony favorable to the defense, stacking juries with jurors biased against the defense, favoritism to the prosecution, prejudgment of cases, oppression, rudeness, contempt, and political ranting. It was this last charge that may have been the most important to Chase's critics. He was accused of using his position on the bench to offer fiery anti-Republican lectures to grand juries. As quoted in John R. Labovitz's book *Presidential Impeachment,* the article of impeachment relevant to this charge stated that Chase, by

> *disregarding the duties and dignity of his judicial character, perverted his official right and duty to address the grand jury . . . for the purpose of delivering . . . an intemperate and inflammatory political harangue . . . [Chase] did . . . by delivering opinions, which, even if the judicial authority were competent to their expression, on a suitable occasion and in a proper manner, were at that time and as delivered by him, highly indecent, extrajudicial, and tending to prostitute the high judicial character with which he was invested, to the low purposes of an electioneering partisan.*

The House managers argued that Chase's statements and speeches from the bench went well beyond his duties as a judge presiding over specific cases. Instead, he used the bench and abused his authority in order to state personal political opinions, lecture his listeners, and influence the outcome of elections.

The Defense: Improper but Not Illegal

Meanwhile, Chase's defense countered all of these accusations by simply stating that, although Chase's behavior on the bench may have been improper, it was not illegal and it certainly did not involve high crimes or misdemeanors. They stressed that impeachable offenses were confined to criminal behavior and law breaking that was performed with criminal and corrupt intent. Even if Chase committed a crime by expressing political opinions from the bench, the defense argued, he did so without criminal intent and therefore could not be impeached.

If no crime was committed for which he could be tried in a criminal court after impeachment and removal, then Chase should not have been impeached in the first place. Error of judgment alone is not impeachable, they claimed. This was especially true if there was no deliberate attempt to achieve corrupt ends by intentionally committing an error of judgment. In effect, Chase was saying that, in his case, without a criminal motive, there can be no crime.

In response to Chase's defense, the House managers argued that no specific, individual impeachable offense had to be proved in order to either charge or convict the judge. Rather, the totality of his "atrocities"—judicial bias and favoritism, lack of objectivity, prejudging of cases, oppressive behavior and language toward the defense, and political speechifying—argued Chase's guilt and merited conviction. They urged the senators to consider the articles of impeachment as a linked chain of evidence, to be viewed as a whole rather than as a collection of individual, freestanding criminal charges.

Failure to Convict

Chase's defense pounced on this recommendation by the House managers, claiming that it showed just how weak the prosecution case was. Because there were no real crimes to consider, they argued, the House managers wanted to distract the senators by creating a vague, overarching impression of bad judgeship. Even if, for argument's sake, the defense conceded that Chase was guilty of being a bad judge, he was still not guilty of an impeachable crime, and the House managers knew it.

Enough senators agreed with Chase's defense and felt uncomfortable with the lack of criminal substance in the House's articles of impeachment. Each of the eight articles brought against Chase was voted down, only three by close margins. One was unanimously rejected. Justice Chase was acquitted.

The importance of the Chase impeachment trial is that it represents a shying away from more politically motivated trial proceedings. It reaffirmed the importance of clearly provable criminal activity and criminal intent as the essential core of any impeachment proceedings. Each article of impeachment should represent a serious crime that would be punishable by criminal courts after the impeachment proceedings. The articles should not simply be a set of vague complaints of wrongdoing that are meant to collectively create a strongly negative impression of an official's character and conduct.

The Chase case helped prove that the Senate took its impeachment responsibilities seriously and understood the gravity of its decisions. In the end, even Republican senators could not in good conscience vote against an irritating, influential, and potentially dangerous enemy—a very vocal and opinionated Federalist judge—if there was no real criminal case against him. This set a very important precedent for loyalty to good government and justice being valued over party loyalty.

PRESIDENT ANDREW JOHNSON

The first presidential impeachment in American history reflects a dynamic similar to that of the Justice Chase case. As in the Chase impeachment, Johnson displayed what many now regard to be objectionable opinions and inappropriate actions in a time of sharp political partisanship. Also as in Chase's case, a politically motivated impeachment that had no serious criminal act at its center was ultimately rejected by senators who placed constitutional considerations and responsibilities over the satisfaction of political revenge.

Johnson's Reconstruction-Era Politics

President Andrew Johnson came to power during an extremely delicate and politically charged period in the nation's history. The Civil War had recently ended, President Abraham Lincoln had been assassinated, and the nation,

President Johnson *(right)* received word that he was being impeached when a sergeant-at-arms *(left)* served him with an impeachment summons at the White House. This illustration of the event was printed in the influential *Harper's Weekly*.

although officially at peace, was still torn by sharp political divisions and animosities. President Johnson was from the border state of Tennessee and had been the only Southern senator to oppose secession from the Union.

Johnson rose to the presidency in 1865, after the war and Lincoln's assassination. This was the period known as Reconstruction. The South—devastated and humbled by war and economic collapse—had to be rebuilt. Its political, cultural, and economic institutions had to be restored, and each former Confederate state had to be gradually drawn back into the Union. To help achieve this, Johnson set up provisional governments in each of the Southern states except Texas. These governments were run by men who had demonstrated and expressed loyalty to the Union and support for abolition of slavery.

Before the Civil War, Johnson had been a Southern Democrat. Most Southern Democrats had been fiercely opposed to the abolition of slavery and the intrusion of the federal government in state affairs. So far, however, Johnson's actions as president reassured and pleased Republicans in Congress. Lincoln had been a Republican, and most members of the party believed passionately in both the Union and its indivisibility (inability to be broken up) and in emancipation (freedom for slaves) and equal rights for African Americans.

Angering the "Radical Republicans"

Trouble began to brew when the civil governments set up by Johnson began to pass "Black Codes" that were designed to keep African Americans at an unfair disadvantage. Johnson did nothing to oppose this. In theory, he believed in emancipation and rights for former slaves, but he was reluctant to force white Southerners to do the right thing. He preferred to believe that they could be trusted to treat African Americans fairly. He also believed that African Americans should not be given the vote immediately. He thought this right should be granted at some later time, when it was politically safer and would not spark a renewed war.

At the same time, former secessionist congressmen were requesting both that their states be readmitted into the Union and that they be given back their seats in Congress. The Republican-dominated Congress resisted their applications and instead passed several measures meant to protect African Americans in the South, including a civil rights bill and an economic relief bill for ex-slaves. President Johnson vetoed these bills, arguing that a Congress in which the full Union was not represented could not pass bills that affected all of the states. If the 11 unrepresented Southern states were refused readmittance into the Union, then Congress could pass no bills that would affect them. From this point on, the Republican Congress and President Johnson were in more or less open warfare.

Johnson's Removal of Edwin Stanton

Things came to a head when, in 1868, Johnson removed his secretary of war, Edwin Stanton, a holdover from Lincoln's cabinet and an important and powerful ally of the so-called "Radical Republicans." These Republicans favored Reconstruction policies that protected African Americans, rewarded pro-Union Southerners, and punished former secessionists by keeping them out of power. The year before, fearing that Johnson would begin to empty the federal government and his cabinet of Lincoln-era Republican appointees, Congress passed the Tenure of Office Act. This act, passed over Johnson's veto, stated that any public officer appointed with the advice and consent of the Senate must remain in that office until a replacement was similarly appointed and approved by the upper house.

When Johnson removed Stanton without the Senate's consent, the House claimed to have the criminal offense it was looking for in order to impeach Johnson (an earlier impeachment attempt in 1867 failed when the House found no substantial criminal actions to provide a basis for the charges). Eleven articles of impeachment were drafted and approved. Most of them concerned Johnson's removal of Secretary Stanton and the authorizing of his replacement in violation of the Tenure of Office Act. One article accused him of treating the office of the presidency with contempt and, through his actions, bringing ridicule and disgrace on it.

Criminal But Not Impeachable?

As had Justice Chase's, Johnson's defense rested mainly on the fact that these charges did not represent impeachable crimes. Johnson claimed that the Tenure of Office Act was unconstitutional, and he intended to argue that before the Supreme Court (in fact, it was partially repealed in 1887 and declared unconstitutional in 1926). Until the Supreme Court passed judgment on its constitutionality, Johnson argued, the real crime would be his enforcement of an act of Congress that he believed to be in violation of the law. Even if the Tenure of Office Act was constitutional, he could not be faulted for misinterpreting the act. He would not have done so with criminal intent; it would have been an honest mistake, his defense argued (rather unconvincingly).

In any case, Johnson's defense claimed, the president's removal of Stanton did no harm to the public or the nation's interests. He may have violated the letter of the law, but he did nothing to endanger the United States and its people. Despite all of the contradictions and hedging of bets in this rather scattershot defense, Johnson's lawyers did raise doubts in some senators' minds and slowed the momentum toward conviction.

The House managers responded by arguing that, even if Johnson's violation of the Tenure of Office Act was not a criminal offense, it was still an impeachable one. The managers ran head-on into the age-old debate about what constitutes an impeachable offense, again questioning whether an offense that would be punished in a criminal court was the only kind of wrongdoing that could get an officer impeached. Their answer was that a crime was not necessary for impeachment. Rather, any act that harmed the public interest, the state, or the common good or was "contrary to the good morals of the office" and was an "offense to common decency" was an impeachable offense. This vague and expansive range of possible offenses was said to include abuse of power, illegitimate seizing of power, and seditious (undermining and challenging of authority) statements by an executive, all of which Johnson was said to have committed in removing Stanton from office without congressional approval.

Stepping Back From the Brink

On May 16, 1868, the Senate took a test vote to see where it stood. The vote was on the eleventh article of impeachment, which was a sort of grab bag that encompassed all of the charges. The votes of 36 senators were needed to convict. Only 35 voted "guilty." Nineteen voted not guilty, including seven Republicans. Voting on the other acts was postponed, so the House managers and Radical Republicans in the Senate could regroup. On May 26, the Senate voted on two other articles. The same 35–19 split occurred.

Admitting defeat, the Radical Republicans moved to adjourn, and the impeachment of President Andrew Johnson came to an abrupt end. Although Johnson wielded his power arrogantly and supported Reconstruction policies that seem objectionable and weak-kneed to the modern eye, there is little doubt that his impeachment was strongly motivated by politics and party outrage. The criminal nature of his offense was never adequately established, and the Radical Republicans quickly abandoned the effort to do so. Instead, they resorted to the most fuzzy of definitions of what an impeachable offense was, potentially opening the door to hasty and ill-considered impeachments of any president who angers, disappoints, or defies Congress. Luckily, the Senate once again backed away from heading down that perilous course.

It would be more than 100 years before the nation faced such a serious crisis of leadership again, and Congress once more found itself preparing to sit in judgment of the president of the United States.

PRESIDENT RICHARD NIXON

Not all impeachment proceedings result in impeachment, much less conviction and removal from office. Sometimes the House's investigation turns up nothing worthy of further action. Sometimes the vote to impeach fails to gain a majority of representatives. Other times, the House may decide to censure (publicly reprimand) the official suspected of wrongdoing rather than enter into the long, exhausting process of an impeachment trial.

In some instances, when impeachment appears to be certain, the official may try to avoid the humiliation of a Senate trial and forcible removal by voluntarily resigning from office. This allows the official to maintain his or her innocence while also preserving some dignity when exiting public life. This was the option chosen by President Richard Nixon when the inevitability of impeachment and the likelihood of conviction became clear to him.

The Watergate Scandal

On June 17, 1972, five men hired by Nixon's reelection committee broke into the Washington, D.C., headquarters of the Democratic National Committee, housed in a hotel-office-apartment complex known as the Watergate. Nixon was a Republican and was preparing for a difficult presidential campaign. His popularity had slipped, mainly because of the United States' ongoing involvement in the Vietnam War, a conflict increasingly opposed by average Americans.

The men who broke into Watergate that night had also broken in three weeks before and planted wiretaps in order to allow Republican operatives to eavesdrop on Democratic election strategizing. They returned a second time to fix some wiretaps that had proven to be faulty and possibly to photograph documents. This time, however, they were caught in the act by a security guard. The Washington, D.C., police arrived and arrested the men. Within hours, a scandal of enormous proportions—now referred to simply as "Watergate"—began to erupt.

The Federal Bureau of Investigation (FBI) took over the case, and the burglars and their activities were traced back to Nixon's reelection committee and many of his key administration staff members. It never became clear how involved, if at all, Nixon himself was in planning and ordering the wiretapping and break-ins. What was certain, however, was that he attempted to organize a cover-up after the burglars' arrest. He and his chief of staff, Bob

The Watergate hotel and office building is shown above. The Democratic National Committee's offices for the 1972 election were located in the Watergate. President Nixon became involved in a scandal when members of his reelection committee broke into the DNC's offices.

Haldeman, were tape recorded discussing the possibility of urging the Central Intelligence Agency (CIA) to obstruct or slow down the FBI's investigation on the grounds of protecting national security. (Nixon secretly taped most of his conversations, a practice that came back to haunt him when he was forced to hand over the tapes to the Senate and a special prosecutor). Later, Nixon did indeed make such a request of the CIA.

The burglars and two of Nixon's shadowy operatives who ran the break-in operation went to trial. They were paid by the reelection committee to plead guilty but reveal nothing. Given this lack of information, the Senate had no choice but to launch its own investigation. The hearings were televised; the American public was riveted. Nixon refused to hand over evidence requested by the Senate, including, most importantly, his office tape recordings. Members of his administration, when pressed, were more forthcoming with information, however, and the revelations that emerged led to the resignations or indictments (charging with a crime), or both, of many of Nixon's most prominent aides.

Impeachment Prevented by Resignation

As things began to unravel, the House of Representatives' Judiciary Committee began an impeachment investigation of President Nixon. On July 27, 1974, the committee voted on the first article of impeachment—obstruction of justice. The article passed on a vote of 27 to 11. Within three days, two more articles that related to Nixon's abuse of power and contempt for Congress were approved. The particular crimes attributed to Nixon in these three articles were wiretapping, misuse of the CIA, perjury (lying under oath), bribery, obstruction of justice, and other abuses of executive power.

Once the tapes of Nixon's conversation with Haldeman were released publicly, most of the Judiciary Committee members who had voted against the articles of impeachment stated that they would no longer oppose them when voted on by the full House. As loyal members of his party began to desert him, Nixon saw the writing on the wall.

On August 8, 1974, President Richard Nixon went on television to announce to Americans that he was resigning from the office of the president. Above, Nixon boards the Marine One helicopter on August 9, the official date of his resignation.

On August 9, 1974, he resigned the presidency before the House had the opportunity to vote on the articles of impeachment prepared by the Judiciary Committee. Richard Nixon escaped impeachment, and, thanks to a pardon by his vice president and successor, President Gerald Ford, he was protected from criminal prosecution. For Nixon, though, an ambitious and proud man, the worst punishment was served: His political career was dead, and he was personally disgraced.

7

THE FUTURE OF THE IMPEACHMENT PROCESS

Every time impeachment proceedings are initiated, especially when the subject of the investigation is the president of the United States, certain age-old questions are revisited and debated. The debate never seems to be resolved definitively. Each new impeachment calls for fresh appraisals of the questions and the possibility of new answers and approaches. What offenses are impeachable? Is there a distinction to be drawn between personal failings and minor errors of judgment or wrongdoing and more serious crimes of office? How much of the impeachment proceedings are motivated by a quest for justice and a desire to protect the nation and the integrity of its government, and how much is motivated by political rivalry, jealousy, and vengeance? With the impeachment of President Bill Clinton in December 1998, all of these questions were again brought to the fore and debated, not only in Congress, but nationwide—in the media, on the Internet, and in offices, schools, and living rooms.

THE WHITEWATER INVESTIGATION

The path to the Clinton impeachment was unusually long and twisting. It started with a real estate deal gone bad. In the 1970s and 1980s, Bill Clinton and his wife, Hillary (now a senator for New York), were two of the principal investors in the Whitewater Development Corporation, a real estate development scheme that failed. The two other investors were later charged with criminal conduct related to Whitewater financial transactions. The Clintons were cleared of similar charges in three separate inquiries.

Questions and suspicions lingered, however. In 1994, in an attempt to put an end to the rumors and finally clear his name, Clinton appointed a special prosecutor (who would be independent of the Clinton administration) to investigate the Whitewater financial dealings. Throughout the most important periods of the six-year investigation, the special prosecutor was Republican lawyer Kenneth Starr. The zeal and persistence with which he investigated Clinton, a Democrat, and pursued other avenues of

THE FUTURE OF THE IMPEACHMENT PROCESS

When news of the Whitewater scandal broke, special prosecutor Kenneth Starr was appointed to investigate President Clinton. Above, Starr talks to reporters for the first time after beginning his investigation.

possible wrongdoing unrelated to Whitewater led many to believe that this was a politically motivated witch hunt of an unusually popular president, one who had rejuvenated the Democratic Party and given it new luster. This suspicion was only compounded when, after six years and $80 million of taxpayer money spent on the investigation, Starr's successor declared that there was insufficient evidence of criminal conduct by either Bill or Hillary Clinton in relation to Whitewater.

Monica Lewinsky (shown here) was an intern at the White House during the Clinton Administration. Lewinsky claimed to have had a relationship with the president, though President Clinton denied it at first.

MONICA LEWINSKY

Starr's investigation had not come up completely empty, however. While the Whitewater investigation was underway, Paula Jones, a former Arkansas state worker, filed a sexual harassment lawsuit against President Clinton that dated back to his years as Arkansas's governor. Starr decided to expand his investigation beyond Whitewater to see what else of a criminal nature could be found regarding Clinton.

In the course of this secondary investigation, Starr received taped telephone conversations from Linda Tripp, an employee in the Pentagon's public affairs office. Tripp used to work in the White House under President

George H. W. Bush but was edged out a year after Clinton took office. The taped conversations were between Tripp and a friend of hers, Monica Lewinsky, a White House intern. In them, Lewinsky described a sexual relationship she had with the president.

In a sworn deposition (testimony taken down in writing) before a grand jury investigating the Paula Jones case, Clinton denied ever having sexual relations with Lewinsky. Later, during a press conference, when news about the allegations began to leak to the press, Clinton again denied publicly that he had had any improper relationship with the White House intern (he would later admit to the relationship). Once Starr received the taped phone conversations from Tripp, he believed that Clinton had committed perjury by lying under oath during the Paula Jones grand jury testimony. He finally had what he believed to be an impeachable offense with which to accuse President Clinton.

CLINTON IS IMPEACHED

Starr delivered the preliminary findings of his investigation to the House of Representatives on September 9, 1998. Many people were struck by how little of it pertained to the Whitewater investigation itself and how much space was devoted to surprisingly graphic details about Clinton's sexual relationship with Lewinsky, again raising questions about the political motivations of Starr's actions.

Although Starr believed that there were 11 grounds for impeachment of President Clinton, the House Judiciary Committee drafted only 4 articles of impeachment—grand jury perjury, civil suit perjury, obstruction of justice, and abuse of power. On December 19, the full House approved two of these four articles, grand jury perjury and obstruction of justice. In both cases, the votes were close and followed party lines—most Republican representatives voted for impeachment, most Democrats voted against it.

LACK OF SENATE SUPPORT FOR CONVICTION

The case was now in the Senate's hands. Once again, the upper house found itself in the difficult and agonizing position of having to decide the fate of a high government official, in this case the president. Once again, each senator had to grapple with his or her conscience regarding questions of right, wrong, justice, partisan politics, the good of the nation, and the relative weight, seriousness, and harmfulness of crimes committed.

In the end, just enough Republicans decided that Clinton's wrongdoing, although not to be excused, did not justify inflicting such harm and disruption to the presidency, the government, and the nation. Clinton was acquitted on both articles of impeachment. On the perjury charge, 10 Republicans voted with all of the Democrats to acquit. On the obstruction of justice charge, 5 Republicans and all the Democrats voted to acquit.

The president's personal popularity may have made it hard for the senators to vote for conviction. The American public gave Clinton high approval ratings even during the impeachment proceedings. Many people were disgusted with the process, feeling that Clinton's crimes were of a

Above, Chief Justice Rehnquist *(top center)* presides over the Senate impeachment trial of President Clinton. In the end, the Senate acquitted Clinton on both articles of impeachment.

personal nature and concerned only himself, his wife, and Lewinsky. They believed that the government had no business getting involved in Clinton's private life, especially if his wrongdoing had nothing to do with his official duties and responsibilities.

Many also suspected that the Republican-dominated House's enthusiasm for impeachment was less a reflection of the representatives' moral outrage than of their frustration with two consecutive presidential election losses and Clinton's enduring popularity. Although Clinton's guilt on the two charges was beyond serious doubt, the gravity of the misbehavior was. Many Americans felt both that these were not impeachable offenses and that the House managers had not proven that they were. They believed that the harmful impact of Clinton's lying under oath on the working of government and the health of the nation was never convincingly established.

As seen in earlier examples, the Senate again showed caution in convicting and removing a public official whose crimes did not seem to many to approach the level of seriousness that merits impeachment. It again resisted strong political pressures to convict and opted instead to deliver a decision that arguably preserved the stability of both the office and the nation. In this sense, the impeachment process was shown to work properly. Members of Congress used their awesome power prudently and allowed the larger concern for the nation's well-being to take precedence over the considerations of party politics.

For many Americans, though, the impeachment of President Clinton indicated that something had gone terribly wrong with the system. They did not believe that justice was served when a man could be repeatedly cleared of wrongdoing during several investigations, only to be publicly shamed by a matter that was intensely private. The impeachment process shook their faith in Congress and its motives at least as much as it harmed their trust in Clinton. There truly were no winners in this matter.

LEARNING FROM THE PAST AND IMPROVING THE IMPEACHMENT PROCESS

Over the years and in the wake of the Clinton impeachment, there have been many proposals to reform and improve the impeachment process. Most of these relate to making the process speedier and more efficient. Some proposals seek to streamline the House investigation and minimize the often long delays between accusation, investigation, and impeachment. For example, the House could rely more heavily on testimony, evidence, and judgments gathered in any trials of the suspect that occurred before the impeachment investigation was instigated. It could hire outside lawyers to help with the more technical and legal aspects of the case, with which even Judiciary Committee members and House managers may not have much familiarity.

Some critics of the impeachment process think that, like the House, the Senate could rely on testimony, evidence, and judgments that result from prior criminal or civil trials of the impeached official to speed up its information gathering and deliberating. It could also more frequently use smaller committees to conduct the trial, allowing it to proceed more quickly while the majority of senators carry on their usual legislative business. These committees could be staffed by senators who have particular experience with impeachment trials or are at least well-versed in matters of trial law. An alternative to this would be to delegate certain trial responsibilities, such as evidence gathering, to outside experts who can perform the tasks more quickly and knowledgably.

It is unlikely that any major reforms or changes to the impeachment process will be made. This is especially true if the proposed changes involve reducing representatives' and senators' full involvement in the process by relying on

"THE INFAMOUS 17"

Below is a list of the 17 federal officials who have been impeached by the House of Representatives. Included are the year of the impeachment, their position in government, and the outcome of the impeachment trial.

Year of Impeachment	Official	Office	Outcome
1799	William Blount	U.S. Senator from Tennessee	Case dismissed
1804	John Pickering	U.S. District Court Judge from New Hampshire	Removed from office
1805	Samuel Chase	Associate Justice, U.S. Supreme Court	Acquitted
1831	James H. Peck	U.S. District Court Judge from Missouri	Acquitted
1862	West H. Humphreys	U.S. District Court Judge from Tennessee	Removed from office
1868	Andrew Johnson	President of the United States	Acquitted
1873	Mark H. Delahay	U.S. District Court Judge from Kansas	Resigned
1876	William W. Belknap	U.S. Secretary of War	Acquitted

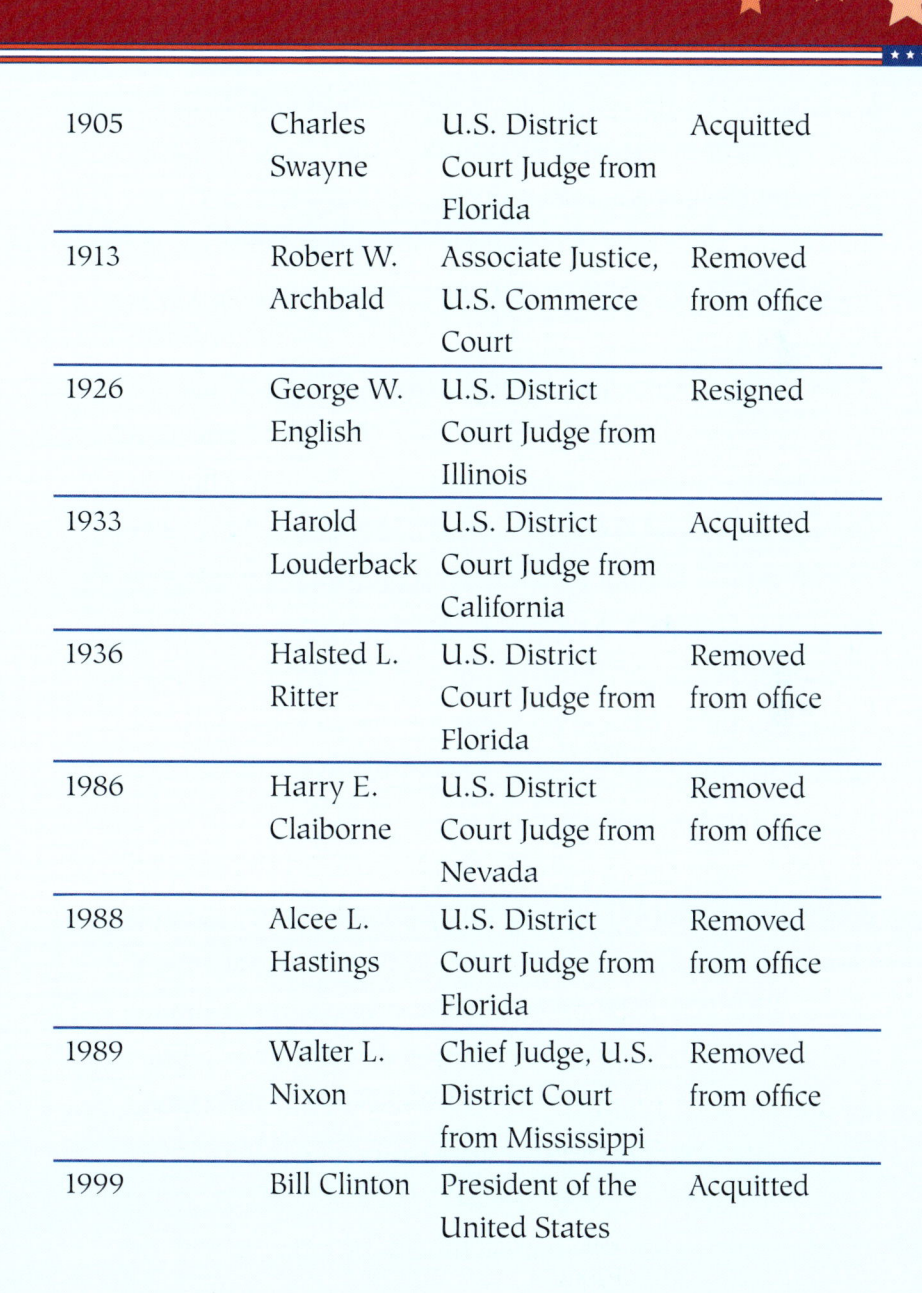

THE FUTURE OF THE IMPEACHMENT PROCESS

1905	Charles Swayne	U.S. District Court Judge from Florida	Acquitted
1913	Robert W. Archbald	Associate Justice, U.S. Commerce Court	Removed from office
1926	George W. English	U.S. District Court Judge from Illinois	Resigned
1933	Harold Louderback	U.S. District Court Judge from California	Acquitted
1936	Halsted L. Ritter	U.S. District Court Judge from Florida	Removed from office
1986	Harry E. Claiborne	U.S. District Court Judge from Nevada	Removed from office
1988	Alcee L. Hastings	U.S. District Court Judge from Florida	Removed from office
1989	Walter L. Nixon	Chief Judge, U.S. District Court from Mississippi	Removed from office
1999	Bill Clinton	President of the United States	Acquitted

outside lawyers and experts to conduct much of the investigation and trial on their behalf. Such a development would probably not sit well with the American public. If a president is to be put on trial, most Americans want him or her to be tried by accountable representatives. If the House and Senate members perform badly during an impeachment trial, the voters can always punish them at election time.

Perhaps the greatest improvement to the process would be an adherence to the guidelines offered by history. The general consensus that emerges from America's experience with impeachment trials is that, in order to ensure a worthwhile trial and a good chance of conviction, the official's crime must be serious, must be related to his or her official duties, and must have compromised the office and the nation. Indeed, the crime must be so grave that members of both parties must be in support of the impeachment. Genuine outrage and fear for the damage that has been done and can be done in the future by the official in question must be felt by a large majority of Congress members, and these feelings must outweigh the natural desire for stability and continuity. Finally, party politics should not be the motivating factor for any impeachment proceeding. It may be present in the process, but it should not set the process in motion. If the misconduct of a public official does not meet these basic criteria, the House and Senate would be well advised to consider alternatives to impeachment, such as censure.

As always with the impeachment process, it will be up to the representatives and senators who face the next

THE FUTURE OF THE IMPEACHMENT PROCESS

congressional investigation and trial to learn the relevant lessons from the Clinton impeachment—and all previous impeachments—in order to conduct a more fair proceeding. By doing so, it can be hoped that they will make the appropriate refinements to the impeachment process and oversee an investigation and trial that are committed to impartial truth and justice and the preservation of integrity in all branches of government.

Impeachment charges bring discredit on the government and its officials and can cause uncertainty and chaos for the nation. Therefore, it is wise that Congress resorts to the process very infrequently. Its rarity also reflects well on the foresight of the Constitution's framers, who hoped that the mere threat of impeachment would keep public officers on the straight and narrow and discourage them from corruption and other temptations that come with power.

The infrequency of impeachment trials also proves the worst fears of its early opponents wrong: In general, Congress has not successfully used impeachment to overthrow unpopular leaders, settle political scores, or engage in party warfare. To their enormous credit, most representatives and senators have approached the proceedings with all the caution, gravity, and reluctance that are appropriate to the significance and unsettling power of the federal impeachment process.

GLOSSARY

acquitted Set free from or cleared of a criminal charge.

agenda A list of things to be done or a political program to carry out.

bicameral A single legislature made up of two chambers, such as the U.S. Congress's House of Representatives and Senate.

bribery Giving money or other gifts in order to influence someone's actions or decisions.

cabinet A council of the chief advisers of a head of state.

civil Relating to the state and its citizens; relating to private rights and lawsuits brought to protect them.

colony A body of people living in a new territory that is governed by a parent state.

Congress The supreme legislative body of the United States, composed of the Senate (the upper house) and the House of Representatives (the lower house).

constitution The basic principles and laws of a nation or state; the document details the government's powers and duties and the rights of citizens.

corruption A loss of integrity or moral values; acting improperly or illegally in order to gain something.

debate Formal discussion or argument about an issue or a proposition.

declaration An official statement of principles.

delegate A person who represents a large body of people, such as a state; a person chosen by a group to represent them at a meeting.

deliberate To think about or discuss issues and decisions very carefully.

executive The branch of government that manages public and national affairs and supervises the execution of laws; in the United States, the chief executive is the president.

federal The central governing authority in a nation made up of several states or territories; relating to a central or national government rather than to individual or state governments.

impeachment The act of accusing or charging someone with a crime or misdemeanor.

indict To charge with a crime, usually after a review of evidence by a grand jury.

initiate To cause the beginning of something; to set something in motion.

judicial Relating to judgment, the administration of justice, or the judiciary (the court system).

legislation Proposed rules created by a decision-making body, like the U.S. Congress or a town council.

legislative The branch of government that is responsible for making laws.

legislature A law-making body.

misdemeanor A misdeed; a crime that is less serious than a felony (a grave crime, with punishment ranging from at least a year in prison to death by execution).

monarchy A system of government based on the rule of a king or queen; the right to rule is passed down through the family rather than through elections or appointments.

New World The land "discovered" by fifteenth- and sixteenth-century European explorers in North and South America.

Parliament The British legislature; the part of the government that passes laws in Great Britain.

partisan Belonging to a certain party; acting according to the dictates of a certain party.

proceedings Events or happenings, often of a legal sort.

prosecution The act of pursuing formal charges against an offender; the individual or group who initiates and conducts the criminal proceedings.

provision A measure taken or specified in preparation for something.

ratify To formally approve, as in a law.

repercussions Consequences; a series of results or effects that follow an event.

treason A betrayal of the nation's trust; the attempt to overthrow one's government or kill or injure its leaders.

tyranny Ruling people through severity, oppression, and cruelty.

BIBLIOGRAPHY

Baumgartner, Jody C., and Naoko Kada. *Checking Executive Power: Presidential Impeachment in Comparative Perspective.* Westport, Conn.: Praeger, 2003.

Berger, Raoul. *Impeachment: The Constitutional Problems.* Cambridge, Mass.: Harvard University Press, 1974.

Black, Charles L., Jr. *Impeachment: A Handbook.* New Haven, Conn.: Yale University Press, 1998.

Brunner, Borgna. "A Short History of Impeachment." Infoplease.com, http://www.infoplease.com/spot/impeach.html.

Dallek, Robert. "Impeachment." MSN Encarta, http://encarta.msn.com/encyclopedia_761577202/Impeachment.html#s1.

"FAQs and Web Resources on the Impeachment Process." American Bar Association, http://www.abanet.org/publiced/impeachment.html.

Gerhardt, Michael J. *The Federal Impeachment Process: A Constitutional and Historical Analysis.* Chicago, Ill.: Chicago University Press, 2000.

Henchey, Brian J. "LII Backgrounder on Impeachment." Legal Information Institute, http://www.law.cornell.edu/background/impeach/impeach.htm. Updated on January 25, 1999.

Hoffer, Peter Charles, and N.E.H. Hull. *Impeachment in America, 1635–1805.* New Haven, Conn.: Yale University Press, 1984.

Labovitz, John R. *Presidential Impeachment.* New Haven, Conn.: Yale University Press, 1979.

BIBLIOGRAPHY

Romney, Matthew R. "The Origins and Scope of Presidential Impeachment." *Hinckley Journal of Politics* 2, no. 1 (Spring 2000): 67–72.

United States Senate. "Impeachment." Senate.gov. http://www.senate.gov/artandhistory/history/common/briefing/Senate_Impeachment_Role.htm.

FURTHER READING

Aaseng, Nathan. *The Impeachment of Bill Clinton.* San Diego, Calif.: Lucent Books, 2000.

Barron, Rachel Stiffler. *Richard Nixon: American Politician.* Greensboro, N.C.: Morgan Reynolds, 2004.

Davis, Kenneth C. *Don't Know Much About History: Everything You Need to Know About American History But Never Learned.* New York, N.Y.: Harper Paperbacks, 2004.

Fernandez, Justin. *High Crimes and Misdemeanors: The Impeachment Process.* New York, N.Y.: Chelsea House, 2000.

Gaines, Ann. *Richard M. Nixon: Our Thirty-Seventh President.* Chanhassen, Minn.: Child's World, 2001.

Giddens, Sandra, and Owen Giddens. *A Timeline of the Constitutional Convention.* New York, N.Y.: Rosen Central, 2003.

Haesly, Richard, ed. *History Firsthand: The Constitutional Convention.* Farmington Hills, Mich.: Greenhaven Press, 2001.

Havelin, Kate. *Andrew Johnson.* Minneapolis, Minn.: Lerner, 2004.

Hughes, Chris. *People at the Center of the Constitutional Convention.* Farmington Hills, Mich.: Blackbirch Press, 2005.

Santella, Andrew. *Impeachment.* New York, N.Y.: Children's Press, 2001.

Shea, Pegi Deitz. *The Impeachment Process.* New York, N.Y.: Chelsea House, 2000.

Web Sites

Government Printing Office (printers of the Congressional Record)
http://www.gpo.gov/

House Judiciary Committee
http://judiciary.house.gov/

The Library of Congress
http://www.loc.gov/index.html

Office of History and Preservation, Office of the Clerk of the House of Representatives
http://clerk.house.gov/

The Richard Nixon Library and Birthplace
http://www.nixonfoundation.org/

Smithsonian Institution, National Museum of American History, Information Office
http://americanhistory.si.edu/index.cfm

United States House of Representatives
http://www.house.gov/Welcome.shtml

United States Senate
http://www.senate.gov/

United States Senate Historical Office
http://www.senate.gov/artandhistory/history/common/generic/Senate_Historical_Office.htm

The White House
http://www.whitehouse.gov/

The William J. Clinton Presidential Library and Museum
http://www.clintonlibrary.gov/

PICTURE CREDITS

PAGE:

9:	AP Images	43:	AP Images/Doug Mills
11:	Library of Congress, cph 3b22815	47:	AP Images
17:	Library of Congress, cph 3c18783	66:	Library of Congress, cph 3c06849
25:	Art Resource, NY	74:	Getty Images
29:	Art Resource, NY	76:	Time & Life Pictures/Getty Images
35:	National Archives/Highlighting by SMGraphics	79:	AP Images/Ron Edmonds
40:	AP Images/Joe Marquette	80:	AP Images
		83:	AP Images

Cover: Library of Congress, LC-USZ62-1732DLC

INDEX

A

Accusation and investigation
  of President Clinton, 78–81
  complaint of misconduct, 39–40, 45, 56, 69
  and criminal trials, 40–41
  and the Judiciary Committee, 9–10, 39–41, 51, 59, 72, 77, 81, 84–85, 88–89
  review of, 41
Adams, John
  impeachment of Blount, 56
African Americans
  equal rights, 67–69
American colonies, 13
  government, 20–21
  impeachment and protest in, 19–22
American Revolution, 24
  aftermath, 12, 21–23, 32
  independence, 22
Archbald, Robert W., 87
  impeachment trial, 51
Arkansas, 80
Articles of Confederation
  weaknesses of, 24–25
Articles of impeachment
  charges, 10, 57, 59, 61–65, 69, 75–76, 81–82, 89
  conviction, 11–12, 50
  debates over, 42, 77
  drafting, 41–42, 69, 81
  reporting to Senate, 42–44, 46, 64
  voting of, 11, 42, 50, 56, 60, 71–72, 75–76

B

Belknap, William W., 86
Berger, Raoul
  Impeachment: The Constitutional Problems, 19, 56
Blount, William, 86
  intrigue and meddling, 55–56
  successful defense, 57–58
Bush, George H.W., 81

C

Candidates, presidential
  election, 30
Central Intelligence Agency (CIA)
  misuse of, 74–75
Charles I, King of England, 20
Charles II, King of England, 20
Chase, Samuel, 86
  acquittal, 64
  crimes, 61–65
  critics, 62–63
  defense at Senate trial, 63–65, 69
  impeachment, 61
Civil Rights
  legislation, 68
Civil War
  events and aftermath, 65, 67
Claiborne, Harry E., 86
Clinton, Bill
  acquittal, 82
  administration, 78
  crimes, accusations of, 81–84
  impeachment, 7, 55, 78, 81–84, 87, 89
  sexual harassment, 80–81
  and the Whitewater scandal, 78–79
Clinton, Hillary
  senator, 78
  and the Whitewater scandal, 78–79
Congress
  censure of, 58, 72
  control of, 68
  debates, 78
  expulsion of, 58
  houses, 13–14, 27, 30, 44, 67, 71, 75, 84, 88–89
  power, 28, 34, 55, 57, 70–71
Constitution
  framers, 54, 89
  impeachment provisions in, 8, 12, 14, 18, 26, 32–33, 38, 45–48, 51, 53–55, 57, 65, 69
  interpretation of, 38–39, 47, 55, 70
  ratification, 33
  violations, 34

INDEX

Constitutional Convention
    delegates to, 24–30, 31–32, 34, 36–37, 54, 59
    impeachment process debates, 18, 25–37, 54, 59
Crimes, impeachable, 18–19, 33–34, 77
    abuse of power, 19, 32, 34, 62–63, 71, 75, 82
    blasphemy, 58–61
    bribery, 16, 18, 33–34, 39, 51, 75
    charged with, 10, 12, 26
    conspiracy, 19, 51
    corruption, 16, 20, 23–24, 31, 34, 51, 60
    drunkenness, 16, 19, 23, 58–61
    extortion, 19, 51
    false income tax returns, 19
    false travel vouchers, 19
    favoritism, 19, 51, 61–62
    foul language, 19, 63
    fraud, 19
    incompetence in office, 16, 23, 61, 64
    insanity, 19, 58–61
    intemperate, inflammatory, and indecent behavior, 61–63
    interfering with elections, 19, 63
    intrigue and meddling, 55–56
    misconduct, 19, 34, 36, 42, 51, 88
    misuse of public funds, 16, 23
    obstruction of justice, 19, 75, 82
    oppression, 16
    perjury, 19, 52, 75, 81–82, 84
    private railroad cars, improper use of, 19
    related to public offices, 14, 23, 27
    treason, 16, 18, 33–34, 39, 56
    tyranny, 20
    unlawful imprisonment, 19
    vulgarity, 16

D

Debates, 26–37
    how trials conducted, 27–30
    presidential impeachment, 30–33
    where trials occur, 27–30
Declaration of Independence, 21
Delahay, Mark H., 86
Delaware
    early constitution, 24
Democratic Party
    members, 73, 78–79, 82
    national committee, 73

E

Edward III, King of England, 15
Electoral College, 30
England
    civil war, 20
    colonies, 19, 21–22, 24, 56
    government, 13–14, 57
    legal system, 14
    loyals, 23
    royal power, 15–16, 18, 20, 23, 32
    Stuart kings, 19–20
English, George W., 86
English Parliament
    Bill of Rights, 14
    Houses of, 13, 15
    members, 16
    role in impeachment, 15–16, 18–20, 23–24
Executive branch, 25
    members, 14, 30, 39
    powers, 31, 33

F

Federal Bureau of Investigation (FBI)
    Watergate investigation, 73–74
Federal Impeachment Process, The (Gerhardt), 51
Federal officeholders
    and impeachment, 8, 33, 36–37, 39, 44–45, 49, 52, 55, 57–58
    types, 55
Federalist Party, 52
    members of, 61–62, 65
Ford, Gerald
    pardon of Nixon, 76
    presidency, 19, 76
    vice presidency, 19, 76
Franklin, Benjamin
    and the Constitutional Convention, 26, 31–32

G

Gerhardt, Michael J.
    The Federal Impeachment Process, 51
Gerry, Elbridge, 31
Government
    branches, 14, 25
    proceedings, 7, 12
    shaping of, 13–14, 21, 24–26
Grand jury investigations
    hearings, 41
    procedure, 10, 12

H

Haldeman, Bob
    and the Watergate scandal, 73–75
Hamilton, Alexander
    and the Constitutional Convention, 26, 28
Harvey, John, 21
Hastings, Alcee L., 86
House Judiciary Committee
    accusation, 39–41, 45, 59, 69, 75, 85, 88
    and the articles of impeachment, 10–12, 42–44, 46, 61, 64, 69, 75–76, 81–83
    delays, 85
    investigation, 9–10, 39–41, 51, 72, 75, 77, 81, 84–85, 87–88
    recommendations, 10, 42, 75–76
    reviews, 40
    subcommittees, 40

INDEX

House of Representatives, 13
  debate, 10
  managers, 10–11, 42–44, 46, 48–49, 51, 62–64, 70–71, 83, 85
  members, 10, 30, 32, 38, 41, 51, 57–58, 69, 88
  number of impeachment proceedings, 54–55
  role in the impeachment process, 8–11, 19, 27–28, 32, 36, 38–45, 56, 72
  Speaker, 32
Humphreys, West H., 86

I

Impeachment
  basic process, 8–9, 77
  confusion, 7–8, 18
  creation of, 22–37
  future of, 77–89
  improvements, 78, 84–85, 88–89
  notable, 54–76
  origins of, 13–21
  responsibility, 8
Impeachment: The Constitutional Problems (Berger), 19, 56

J

James I, King of England, 20
James II, King of England, 20
Johnson, Andrew, 86
  angering "Radical Republicans," 67–68
  "black codes," 67–68
  crimes, 70–72
  defense, 69–71
  impeachment, 55, 69, 71
  presidency, 65, 67
  Reconstruction-era politics, 65, 67
  removal of Edwin Stanton, 68–71
  vetoes, 68–69
  vice presidency, 65
Jones, Paula
  sexual harassment case, 80–81
Judicial branch
  common law, 14
  power, 28
Justices and judges
  and impeachment, 8, 14, 39, 51–52, 55, 57–65

L

Labovitz, John R.
  Presidential Impeachment, 31, 62
Latimer, William, 15
Lewinsky, Monica
  and President Clinton, 80–81, 83
Lincoln, Abraham
  assassination, 65, 67
  cabinet, 68–69
Louderback, Harold, 87
  impeachment trial, 51
Lyons, Richard, 15

M

Madison, James
  and the Constitutional Convention, 26, 28, 31, 34
Magna Carta, 14
Mason, George, 31
Massachusetts
  representatives, 31, 56
Medieval England
  impeachment in, 14–16, 18–19
  Parliament powers, 15–16, 18–19

N

Native American
  political affairs, 55–56
New Hampshire
  judges, 58
New Jersey
  delegates, 28
New Jersey Plan, 28
New York
  early constitution, 23
  representatives, 78
Nixon, Richard M.
  administration, 73, 75
  crimes, 75
  impeachment threat, 7, 19, 72
  pardon, 76
  reelection committee, 73–74
  resignation, 19, 59, 72, 75–76
  and Watergate, 73–75
Nixon, Walter L., 87
  conviction of perjury, 52
North Carolina
  early constitution, 23

O

"Origins of Scope of Presidential Impeachment, The" (Romney), 23–24

P

Paterson, William, 28
Peck, James H., 86
Pennsylvania
  early constitution, 23
Pentagon, 80
Philadelphia, Pennsylvania
  Constitutional Convention in, 24
Pickering, John, 86
  conviction, 58, 61
  drunkenness, blasphemy and insanity, 58–61
President, 25
  appointments, 28, 57, 69
  cabinet members, 8–9, 14, 39, 55, 57
  and complaints of misconduct, 39
  election, 30
  and impeachment, 7–8, 10, 12, 26, 30–33, 35–36, 39, 45–46, 48, 50, 52, 57, 65, 67–76, 77, 81–82
  powers, 33
  removal from office, 7

Presidential Impeachment (Labovitz), 31, 62
Punishments, 44
    debates over, 34
    early, 19, 23
    forbidden to hold future offices, 23, 27–28, 37, 50
    removal from office, 12, 14, 23, 27–28, 37, 50, 56, 72

R

Randolph, Edmund
    and the Virginia Plan, 27–28
Republican party
    members, 61–62, 65, 67, 69, 71, 73, 78, 82–83
    radical, 67–69, 71
Resignation
    escape from impeachment, 55, 59, 72, 75–76
Richard II, King of England, 16, 18
Ritter, Halsted L., 87
Romney, Matthew
    "The Origins of Scope of Presidential Impeachment," 23–24

S

Senate, 13
    hearings, 74–75
    members, 30, 32, 52, 57–58, 67, 69, 78, 82, 84, 88
    role in the impeachment process, 8–9, 10–12, 28–30, 32, 35, 45–53, 55–56, 65
Senate trials
    absence during, 47, 51, 88
    after removal, 56–58
    appeals, 52–53
    and Clinton, 82–84
    conviction in, 50–53, 58, 61
    debate and deliberations, 11, 49–50, 88
    infrequency of, 89
    procedures, 8, 26, 30, 32, 35–36, 46–49, 60, 72, 85
    reading of articles of impeachment, 42–44, 46, 64, 70–72
    revisal of the rules, 46
    special committees, 47–49
Slavery
    abolition of, 67–68
Southern Reconstruction
    policies, 67–69, 71

Spain
    territories, 56
Stanton, Edwin
    removal of, 68–71
Starr, Kenneth
    investigation, 78–81
State
    constitutions, 22–24
    governments, 26
    impeachment processes, 22–24, 27
    judges, 24, 28
Sumners, Hatton, 51
Supreme Court, 14
    appeals to, 52–53
    chief justices, 8, 10, 32, 46, 50
    justices of, 28–29, 52–53, 61
    power, 26, 28
    rulings, 46, 70
    states, 24
Swayne, Charles, 87

T

Tennessee
    representatives, 55, 67
Tenure of Office Act, 69–70
Texas
    representatives from, 51, 67
Tripp, Linda
    telephone conversations, 80–81

V

Vice President, 14
    and impeachment, 8, 33, 39, 57
    to president, 12, 50
Vietnam War, 73
Virginia
    delegates, 27–28, 31
    early constitution, 24
Virginia Plan, 28
Voting for impeachment and convictions
    in the House of Representatives, 10, 42, 56, 59, 72, 75–76, 82
    how many required, 32, 35–37, 50
    in the Senate, 11–12, 49–52, 56–57, 59–61, 64, 71–72

W

Watergate scandal, 73–75
Whitewater Development Corporation, 78
Whitewater investigation
    events of, 78–81

ABOUT THE AUTHOR

JOHN MURPHY is a writer who lives and works in New York City. He has a master's degree in English literature, with a specialty in medieval Irish and English poetry. Murphy has written and edited numerous books on politics, government, history, and American studies for middle- and high-school readers. He is particularly interested in the ancient, medieval, and colonial underpinnings of American law and government.